A CELEBRATION OF
SCOTLAND

A CELEBRATION OF
SCOTLAND

Janice Anderson

Regency House 🏮 Publishing Ltd.

Pages 2 -3: Loch Leven, with the Pap of Glencoe rising beyond the loch's southern shore.

These pages: Islands of the Outer Hebrides: looking towards Barra from South Uist.

Published in 1996 by
Regency House Publishing Limited
The Grange
Grange Yard
London SE1 3AG

Copyright © 1996 Regency House Publishing Limited

ISBN 1 85361 444 0

Printed in China

Contents

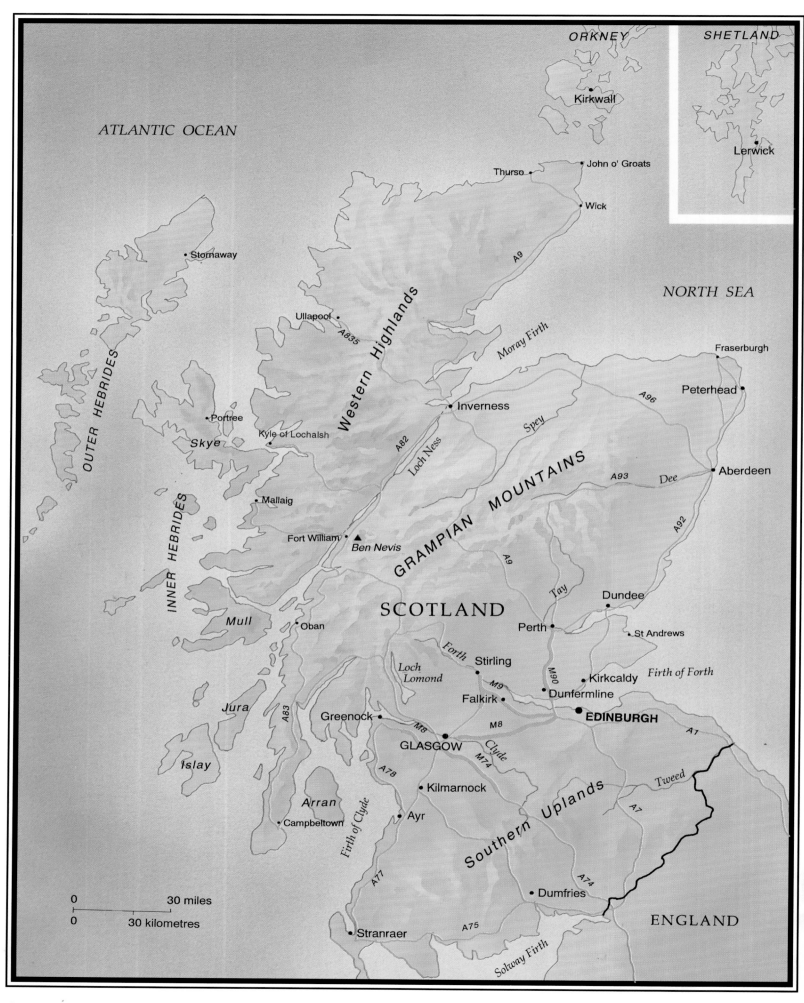

ATLANTIC OCEAN

ORKNEY

SHETLAND

Lerwick

Kirkwall

Thurso • John o' Groats

Wick

NORTH SEA

Stornaway

A9

Western Highlands

Ullapool •

A835

Fraserburgh

Moray Firth

Peterhead

Portree •

Inverness

Spey

A96

Skye

Kyle of Lochalsh

A82

Loch Ness

GRAMPIAN MOUNTAINS

A93

Dee

Aberdeen

Mallaig •

A92

INNER HEBRIDES

OUTER HEBRIDES

Fort William •

▲
Ben Nevis

A9

Tay

Dundee

SCOTLAND

Mull

Oban

Perth

St Andrews

Forth

Stirling

Firth of Forth

Loch
Lomond

M9

M90

Kirkcaldy

Jura

A83

Greenock •

Falkirk

Dunfermline

EDINBURGH

A1

GLASGOW

M8

M8

Clyde

M74

Tweed

Islay

A78

Kilmarnock

A7

Arran

Firth of Clyde

Ayr

Southern Uplands

A74

Campbeltown •

A77

Dumfries

0   30 miles

0   30 kilometres

A75

ENGLAND

Stranraer

Solway Firth

6

Introduction

Scotland is a very bonnie country. There are any number of picture books, glossy calendars and guide books to tell us so. But Scotland is much more than the tartan-draped idyll that the tourist offices would have us believe, and it is the main aim of this book to describe the country as it is, in all its variety.

Every part of the country is visited, from the green, wooded valleys of the Border country to the wild country of mountain and peat bog in Sutherland, from the pretty fishing and holiday villages along the Solway Firth to the quiet hamlets of Orkney and Shetland.

While much is made in this book of the beauty of the land of Scotland, famous throughout the world for its mountains and glens, rivers and lochs, the people who, over the centuries, made a nation out of the remote lands of northern Britain also have a big part to play in it. And not just the great names of Scottish history, such as Robert the Bruce, William Wallace, Mary, Queen of Scots, or Sir Walter Scott. They all made a big contribution to Scotland's history, of course, but so did the nameless Picts, Celts, Norsemen and others who left signs of their occupation in many parts of the country, and their brochs, stone circles and settlements are described here

alongside the castles and great houses of kings and queens, lords and commoners.

The book also visits the great cities and the small towns and villages of Scotland, looks at its industries, from North Sea oil to whisky, and takes pride in the contribution to Scotland's literary greatness of such writers as Robert Burns, Sir Walter Scott and John Buchan.

In celebrating a country which, though no longer an independent state, is very much a nation, with its independent legal, educational, local government and church systems, this book aims to be a summary of what it means to be a Scot. We can't hope to better Sir Walter Scott, Scotland's first great public relations man, of course, so perhaps he should have the last word on the matter. This is how he summed it up in *The Lay of the Last Minstrel* in 1805:

O Caledonia! stern and wild
Meet nurse for a poetic child!
Land of brown heath and shaggy wood,
Land of the mountain and the flood,
Land of my sires! what mortal hand
Can e'er untie the filial band
That knits me to thy rugged strand?

ABOVE
The Paps of Jura dominate the southern half of Jura, one of the islands of the Inner Hebrides. The romantically named An Oir (Mountain of Gold) is, at 792 metres (2576 feet), the highest of the Paps of Jura.

Chapter One
The Borders

There are two things to establish about Scotland's Border country at the outset. First, despite the long centuries of fighting Norsemen, Englishmen, cattle rustlers and each other, the people who live here have not given any war-like aspect to the land. This is serenely calm, rolling hill country and moorland, broken by the valleys of fine, tree-edged rivers where salmon leap and trout flick through the sparkling waters, and where many of the well-ordered farms have the aspect of parkland surrounding an elegant mansion. There are many of the latter, too, built round the old defensive peel towers once the need for strong defences had gone.

Second, you are definitely in Scotland here. This is not some sort of Anglo-Scotia, where people and culture from both sides of the Border have merged into something which is not clearly either. There is no need of signs saying 'Scotland' to tell people that they have crossed the Border north of Berwick-upon-Tweed, or at Coldstream, Carter Bar or Gretna.

While the south-east corner of Dumfries and Galloway comes into this chapter, because the

Border has its western end here at Gretna on the Solway Firth, most of Scotland's Border country falls within the bounds of the modern local government region called Borders. The Borders region takes in four historic shires in the south-east of the country, Peebles, Berwick, Selkirk and Roxburgh. The names of the four shires are also held by four places. Peebles and Selkirk are good-sized thriving communities, Roxburgh is an unremarkable village several miles from the site of the old town and once-mighty castle of Roxburgh, whose ruins stand on a mound between the Teviot and Tweed rivers west of Kelso, and Berwick-upon-Tweed is no longer in Scotland, having ended up on the wrong side of the net after centuries of being a kind of shuttlecock in the Anglo-Scottish wars which ravaged this quiet countryside.

For many centuries the Border lands were a battleground fought over not just by armies of Scotland and England but by sheep-stealers and cattle-raiders, called Border reivers, and landowners seeking self-aggrandizement both north and south of the disputed Border. The

'official' armies tended to cross to and fro nearer the eastern end of the Border, which is why Berwick-upon-Tweed was one of the most heavily fortified towns in medieval Britain. Even so, the town changed hands thirteen times between 1147 and 1482, when Richard, Duke of Gloucester, later Richard III, took it finally for England. Another much-used crossing in the days before bridges was the ford at the Tweed's confluence with Leet Water; today, Coldstream, the village which grew up by this ford, is still a main entry point into Scotland from England, via a main road from Newcastle-upon-Tyne.

Nearer the western end of the Border country, round Teviotdale and Liddesdale, the land was actually called the 'Debatable Land' and was claimed by both Scotland and England from medieval times right up to the 18th century. This was the end of the Border where the cattle rustlers and sheep stealers tended to operate. Today, the names of Border reivers like Johnnie Armstrong and his kinsman William Armstrong, subject of Walter Scott's romantic 'Ballad of Kinmont Willie', live on in story and ballad in their former hunting grounds round Teviotdale and the wildly beautiful Liddesdale, and the remains of grim castles, peel towers and once-beautiful abbeys mark the countryside all the way from Liddesdale in the west across to the North Sea coast in the east.

These places, from the gaunt ruins of castles like Hermitage, set in the bracken-trimmed hill country of Liddesdale, and Roxburgh, away to the east near Kelso, to the four great abbeys founded in the 12th century — Jedburgh, Kelso, Melrose and Dryburgh — stand out in great contrast to the quiet, gentle, heather- and bracken-covered hill country which makes up most of the Borders today. They also make an interesting contrast with the many elegant country houses, including Floors Castle, Mellerstain House, Bowhill House and numerous others, which began to be built in the Borders, often around existing peel towers, in the 18th century, when the centuries-long fighting was over.

It is as if history has decided that, with so much turbulence behind it, the Border country deserves some quiet: even the North Sea oil industry which has brought changes to so many parts of Scotland since the early 1970s has, outwardly at least, passed the Borders by. In much of the Borders region sheep and cattle grazing is still as important a business now as it was in medieval times. Sheep remain the basis of the woollen cloth and knitwear industries of the Borders as they have been for centuries, with the weaving industries in towns like Galashiels and Hawick able to trace their origins back over seven centuries and more.

The Borders are very much hill country, not the dramatic peaks and great mountains separated by lonely glens which mark the Highlands, but something much more gentle. The Southern Uplands, a range of green and purple rounded peaks and moorland stretching westwards from a line between Edinburgh and Peebles, one of the most noteworthy Borders towns, mark the northern edge of the Borders,

LEFT
Coldstream's fine bridge dates from 1766 and was one of several built in Scotland by John Smeaton in the 18th century. It replaced the ford which for centuries had been used for crossing the Tweed into England.

BELOW
Heavily restored though they are, the ruins of Hermitage Castle are still an impressive sight beside Hermitage Water north of Liddesdale. The castle dates back to the 14th century, when it was taken from its builders, the Soulis family of dubious reputation, by the Douglases. The Douglases later exchanged the castle for Bothwell Castle near Glasgow, which is why it was owned by Mary, Queen of Scots' lover, James, Earl of Bothwell in 1566 when the Queen made her famous ride from Jedburgh to Hermitage Castle to see Bothwell, who had been wounded in a Border skirmish.

OVERLEAF
Floors Castle, seat of the dukes of Roxburghe, near Kelso.

along with the Pentland, Moorfoot and
Lammermuir hills south of Edinburgh, while to
the south the Cheviot Hills and the valleys of
several rivers mark the southern edge.

Probably the most famous of the Border
country's hills, because they have figured so
largely in the myth and legend of the region, are
the heather-covered Eildon Hills, a triple-peaked
volcanic range rising up behind the town of
Melrose in the central part of the Tweed Valley.
The Romans called these hills Trimontium, and
built a fort near Newstead at their base and a
signal station on one of the summits, demolishing
the ramparts of an Iron Age hill fort built by a
people called the Selgovae, in the process.

Legend has it that the Eildon Hills were
originally one hill, cleft in three by the wizard
Michael Scot to settle an argument with the devil.
It was also on these hills, so another legend says,
that Thomas of Ercildoun met the Queen of
Elfland under the Eildon Tree and was carried off
to her country for seven years; today, a stone
beside the A6091 road marks the supposed site of
the Eildon Tree. Sir Walter Scott, who bought a
farm three miles west of Melrose which he rebuilt
into the splendid Abbotsford, set his great epic
poem, *The Lay of the Last Minstrel*, around the
Eildon Hills.

Highest points in the Borders hill country are
840-metre (2750-foot) Broad Law and the 20
metres (70 feet) lower Dollar Law in the craggy,
rugged moorland country in the west of the region
where the River Tweed rises.

While the Tweed, famous for its salmon
fishing and for having given its name to the
woollen cloth manufactured here, is the major
river of the region, flowing through three of its
most important towns, Peebles, Melrose and
Kelso, and with many tributaries flowing into it, it
is far from being the only one, for this is a region
of many rivers and burns. In the west and south of
the region there are the Esk, Liddel Water, a long
stretch of which forms part of the line of the
Border in the west, and the Teviot, all of which
have given their names to the dales down which
they flow. In the west, another river, the Sark,
marks the Border's line past Gretna and so to the
coast. To the north, Yarrow Water flows out of
the region's biggest loch, St Mary's Loch, down
a fine valley to join the Tweed a few miles
beyond Selkirk.

Unlike the rest of Scotland, especially the
Highlands, the Border country is not famous for
its lochs. Indeed, St Mary's Loch and the Loch of
the Lowes are the only two of any size – and even
they were one stretch of water in their youth – and
there are several reservoirs, including the Talla,
Fruid and Megget reservoirs. South of the Talla
Reservoir and St Mary's Loch, Loch Skeen, a
corrie loch, lies high up in the Southern Uplands.
The burn that runs out of it drops via the famous

Grey Mare's Tail 200 feet into space, making the most spectacular waterfall in Scotland outside the Highlands.

St Mary's Loch and the Loch of the Lowes lie in a glacial basin at the heart of the land once covered by the extensive Ettrick Forest, a rugged countryside and a royal hunting preserve but today mostly peaceful moorland where sheep graze, which has inspired some of Scotland's finest poets, including Sir Walter Scott, Robbie Burns and James Hogg, the 'Ettrick Shepherd', as well as William Wordsworth, exploring over the Border from his beloved Lake District. James Hogg was born in Ettrick and was virtually uneducated, unlike both Scott and Burns. What he shared with Robbie Burns was a wonderful empathy with the traditional ballads and stories of the Borders, which found expression in some very fine poetry.

Once a refuge for hunted Covenanters and fierce Border reivers, the glens and hills of the Ettrick Forest now provide quiet grazing for sheep and cattle and fine walking for ramblers. The walk which circumnavigates St Mary's Loch, most of it on footpaths and forestry roads, has been planned to take in as many as possible of the places of particular interest here. Walkers can see the ruins of the impressive Dryhope Tower, once the home of the notorious Border reiver Wat Scott of Harden; the fine statue of James Hogg, his sheepdog Hector at his feet, which looks towards the Loch of the Lowes; and even Tibbie Shiels Inn, named after its first landlady, at the southern end of St Mary's Loch, where James Hogg was a regular customer, often having long talking and drinking sessions here with the much more cultured and sophisticated Walter Scott. 'He was a gey sensible man for a' the nonsense he wrat,' remarked Tibbie Shiels of James Hogg early in the 19th century. Today, the inn's customers are more likely to be walkers and yachtsmen from the sailing club based on the lochside than poets.

The river that flows from the north-eastern end of St Mary's Loch is the Yarrow: hence the name 'the Flower of Yarrow' given to Walter Scott of Harden's famously beautiful wife, Mary.

Away on the eastern edge of the Ettrick Forest is Selkirk, rising on a hillside above another river of the area, the Ettrick, a Mecca for salmon and trout fishermen. Selkirk has been a manufacturing town for nearly four centuries, specializing in the weaving of woollen cloth.

Selkirk makes a fine base for visiting the many places of interest around it, including Bowhill in the Yarrow valley, which has for centuries been the home of the Scotts of Buccleuch, though the present fine house with its superb art collection was begun only in the late 18th century.

Selkirk comes really alive in June when the town holds it annual Common Riding; horsemen carrying symbols of their town's independence ride the surrounding countryside to commemorate the heroic part played by the men of Selkirk in the disastrous Battle of Flodden in 1513, in which James IV was killed and the flower of the Scottish Army destroyed.

While Selkirk claims that its Common Riding is the biggest mounted gathering in Europe, other Border towns also hold sizeable Common Ridings every summer, when the boundaries of their towns are ridden by local people, to the accompaniment of brass and pipe bands, revelry and merrymaking. The Common Ridings of the Borders today are used, like the Games of the Highlands, as a way of gathering local people together to celebrate their lives and localities. Their historic significance lies in the fact that it was once essential for every town in the Borders to be able

ABOVE
Scott's View, above the Tweed, is so called
because it was Sir Walter Scott's favourite view
of Old Melrose and the Eildon Hills beyond.
Here, Scott's funeral cortege paused before
taking the great novelist's body to its last resting
place in Dryburgh Abbey.

LEFT
St Mary's Loch, another beauty spot often visited
by Sir Walter Scott, was also home territory for
James Hogg, the Ettrick Shepherd, who farmed
near the loch for several years.

to defend its territory; in time, the important
business of marking a town's boundaries became
formalized into a ceremony of 'riding the bounds'.

Among Border towns which have Common
Ridings are Duns, Galashiels, Hawick, Jedburgh,
Langholm and Lauder. Peebles, an attractive town
on the Tweed to the north-west of Selkirk,
includes a Common Riding in its annual Beltane
Fair, a descendant of the great Celtic festival of
the sun marking the beginning of summer.
Outside the week of its Beltane festival in June,
Peebles is a quiet town, which is just as it should
be, for Peebles' two great claims to fame are both
quiet matters: the fine quality of the salmon
fishing in the Tweed and the fact that William
and Robert Chambers, brothers and founders of
the fine 19th-century Edinburgh publishing firm,
Chambers, were born here. The great Chambers
Dictionary still goes strong, with new editions

being published every decade or so.

That Peebles has known more warlike times
is attested to by Neidpath Castle, perched on a
rocky outcrop above the Tweed just a mile from
the town. Neidpath, dating from the 14th century
and with walls nearly 3.5 metres (11 feet) thick, is
a finely preserved example of the peel (or 'pele')
tower which provided defensive fortifications on
both sides of the Border for centuries. The word
comes from the Latin 'palus', meaning 'palisade'
and sums up its purpose perfectly.

Traquair House, six miles or so downstream
from Neidpath near Innerleithen, was once a peel
tower also, though the ancient tower is very much
hidden within the 17th-century building which
predominates in the house today. Thought to be
the oldest continuously inhabited house in
Scotland, Traquair has in its long history been
visited by many monarchs of both Scotland and

LEFT
Riders taking part in Selkirk's annual Common Riding, the biggest of the numerous ridings which take place in the Borders every year. Once an important marking of territory in times of frequent battles with English raiders from over the Border, the Common Ridings are today festive occasions.

BELOW
Neidpath Castle, near Peebles on the Tweed, is a peel tower dating from the 14th century.

RIGHT
Smailholm Tower, a fine 16th-century peel tower west of Kelso. The tower's romantically isolated setting near a small loch did much to fire the imagination of the young Walter Scott who spent several summer holidays at nearby Sandyknowe Farm.

England, including Mary, Queen of Scots who came here with her husband and baby son in 1566. Another fine example of a peel tower in this part of the Borders is Smailholm Tower near St Boswells, west of Kelso, whose romantic history so fired the imagination of the young Walter Scott.

Medieval Border Scots were so sure that they were going to be attacked by the English at some time or other that they often did not bother to build strong family dwellings, making do with posts and branches or other forms of wattle and daub which could be rebuilt quickly once the attackers had gone and the defenders could emerge from their towers. This is one reason why so many Border towns and villages have few really ancient buildings, apart from the church and the local stronghold. Hardly a trace remains of Old Roxburgh, for instance, though it was an important medieval town near the mighty fortress of Marchmont, later called Roxburgh Castle, where Alexander II was married and where his son, Alexander III, was born. In 1460, James II was killed by a bursting cannon while attacking Roxburgh Castle, which had been held by the English for over a century. James' grieving widow urged the Scots on to get rid of the English then had the castle and the town surrounding it entirely demolished so that they could never serve again as a base for the English.

The little that is left of Roxburgh Castle can be seen today on the south bank of the Tweed, opposite Kelso, far downstream of Peebles and much nearer the Border. Kelso is among the most attractive of the Border towns, with a fine cobbled market square surrounded by buildings dating back to the 18th century. Near the town is the elegant 18th-century mansion, Floors Castle, seat of the dukes of Roxburghe. A yew tree in the

grounds at Floors is said to mark the site where James II was standing at the seige of Roxburgh Castle when the exploding cannon killed him.

Like Floors Castle, Mellerstain House, seven miles north-west of Kelso, was designed by Scotland's most famous architects and designers, the Adam family. William Adam began both houses, but where Floors was given its final form by W. H. Playfair in the 19th century, Mellerstain House was very much an Adam family creation, for what William Adam began in 1725 his son Robert Adam completed in 1778. Together, they made what has been called the finest and most beautifully proportioned 18th-century mansion in Scotland. As impressively designed and embellished inside as out, Mellerstain House today sits above elegant Italian terraced gardens at the heart of a beautifully wooded formal park.

Kelso was one of the places chosen by David I as a site for the abbeys he founded in the Scottish Borders in the 12th century, at Kelso, Jedburgh and Melrose. (The Borders' fourth 12th-century abbey, Dryburgh, was founded by Hugh de Morville, Constable of Scotland.) Kelso's abbey was one of the largest and richest of the Borders abbeys, wielding great influence for several centuries. Although it was virtually destroyed by the English Earl of Hertford in 1545, during Henry VIII's 'rough wooing' of Mary, Queen of Scots, there is still much fine Norman and early-Gothic work to be seen in what is left, especially on the facade of the north-west transept.

Better preserved is the abbey at Melrose, another quietly attractive town further up the Tweed. Melrose Abbey, founded by David I in 1136, was the first Cistercian monastery in Scotland and achieved lasting fame because of its place in Walter Scott's hugely successful poem, *The Lay of the Last Minstrel*. Robert the Bruce's heart was said to have been laid to rest by the high altar in Melrose Abbey, but it has never been found.

Just short distances from Melrose are two other places connected with Scott, Dryburgh to the south and Abbotsford to the west. Despite his connection with Melrose Abbey, Sir Walter Scott was himself laid to his final rest in Dryburgh Abbey, partly because his family, who had once owned the lands on which the abbey ruins stood, retained the right to 'stretch their bones' there. Also 'stretching his bones' in Dryburgh Abbey is Earl Haig, the World War I general and Allied commander. Today, the considerable and impressive ruins of Dryburgh Abbey stand amidst trees in an idyllic spot on the banks of the Tweed.

Abbotsford, two and a half miles west of Melrose, was an insignificant farmhouse called Clartyhole (meaning 'muddy place') when Sir Walter Scott bought it in 1811. By the time he died in 1832, the simple building had been transformed into a flamboyantly turreted pile in

mock baronial style, complete with armoury, library and museum, and much more suited to Scott's reputation as Britain's most famous historical novelist. Even its new name derived from history, for this place on the Tweed had been the point at which the monks of Melrose had crossed the river.

The fourth of the great abbeys of the Borders region is to be found in Jedburgh, just 10 miles

north of the Border, where Carter Bar is the crossing point on the A68. Jedburgh is perhaps the most historically important of all the Border towns. Nearly 2000 years ago, the Romans began the southern end of their Dere Street here; some time in the 9th century AD a Christian chapel was built here. Early in the 12th century, David I replaced the chapel with a priory, which became the great abbey, whose ruins still dominate the town, in 1147. Round about 1300, Jedhart, as the town was known then, became a royal burgh.

Jedburgh Abbey is a striking red sandstone ruin, standing above Jed Water, its great tower, rebuilt in 1500, rising proudly above the long line of the nine-bayed nave. While much of the stonework in Jedburgh Abbey dates from the 12th century and later, examples of stone carving from two centuries and more before, now in the abbey's museum, are evidence of the age of this important religious site.

Jedburgh's once strategically important castle was also a favoured royal residence. The wedding feast which followed Alexander III's second marriage in Jedburgh Abbey in 1285 was held here. Legend tells of a ghost at the feast, prophesying violent death for the king and disaster for Scotland; sure enough, a year later Alexander III was dead and Scotland had plunged into the several centuries of turmoil that preceded the stabilizing of the monarchy under the Stuarts. The castle was reduced to rubble early in the 15th century to keep it out of English hands, but its foundations were given a new use in 1825 when the Castle Jail was built on them. Today there is an interesting museum of local life in the Castle Jail – but no ghost.

The most romantic story surrounding Jedburgh, worthy of a place in one of Scott's Waverley novels, concerns Scotland's tragic Mary, Queen of Scots. She came to Jedburgh for the assizes in 1566, choosing to stay, so it is said, in the only house in the town with indoor sanitation (now Queen Mary's House, off the High Street and open to the public in the summer months). While at Jedburgh Mary heard that her lover, James, Earl of Bothwell, was lying seriously wounded at Hermitage Castle, nearly 20 miles away beyond Hawick. Impetuously, Mary rode from Jedburgh to Hermitage and back in one day, falling dangerously ill herself on her return. 'Would that I had died at Jedburgh', the Queen was heard to sigh during her long captivity in England.

ABOVE
An attractive corner in Jedburgh, which was for several centuries a strategically important Border town built round a great castle and an abbey. Today, the abbey, an impressive ruin, still attracts visitors to Jedburgh, but the castle has disappeared, its foundations used for a prison built early in the 19th century.

RIGHT
All that remains of Melrose Abbey, founded early in the 12th century by David I for a group of Cistercian monks from Rievaulx Abbey in Yorkshire. Its position close to the Border meant that the abbey was destroyed and rebuilt several times, most notably by Robert the Bruce. Its final destruction was at the hands of the English Earl of Hertford in 1545.

Mary, Queen of Scots' reign in Scotland came to an end within a year of her Jedburgh escapade. Early in 1567, her husband Darnley was murdered and within months Mary had married Bothwell, suspected by many of having been implicated in Darnley's death. Not long afterwards Mary was forced to abdicate in favour of her infant son James. By 1568, she had fled to England.

With the flight of this tragic queen, much of the romance departs from the story of the Scottish Borders. Her presence is remembered right across these lands, at Dunbar Castle on the east coast, where she and her husband Darnley took refuge after the murder of David Rizzio and where she stayed again after her marriage to the Earl of Bothwell, at Jedburgh and Hermitage Castle, at Traquair House and finally, at Dundrennan, west of the Border, from where she crossed the Solway Firth to England.

It was given to Sir Walter Scott, an Edinburgh advocate, Clerk of the Signet and sheriff of Selkirk, to bring romance back to the Borders in triumph, using much of the Border country and its ballads and legends in his own poetry and the long series of the romantically historical Waverley novels.

TOP
The magnificent façade of the north-west transept of Kelso Abbey, another of the abbeys founded in the Borders by David I. For centuries the monks of Kelso wielded great influence in the Borders; the last of them died in the abbey when it was razed by the Earl of Hertford in 1545.

ABOVE
Once the site of an important fortress, Dunbar is today a holiday town. Cromwell used stones from the razed fortress to rebuild the harbour.

RIGHT
A beautifully wooded stretch of the River Tweed.

Writers' Inspiration

Scotland's Borders hold a particular place in literary history, because of the number of writers who have made major contributions to literature, especially poetry and prose fiction, who were either born in the southern lands of Scotland or did much of their best work there. Walter Scott, James Hogg, Robbie Burns, John Buchan and Hugh MacDiarmid, who lived near the small town of Biggar, are among the writers who found inspiration in the Border land of Scotland. There are many places associated with them, including their homes, inns which they frequented and buildings they wrote about, which may be visited in the Borders today.

Sir Walter Scott

Right at the top of the literary pilgrim's visiting list is Abbotsford, Sir Walter Scott's home for twenty years. Born in Edinburgh into an academic family with connections with the law, Scott spent much of his childhood at his grandfather's farm, Sandyknowe, near Kelso, thus getting to know the Border country early in his life. He took a keen interest in the literature and history of his country from childhood. His first major work, *The Border Minstrelsy*, was published in 1802 and 1803; more verse romance, *The Lay of the Last Minstrel*, came two years later and brought him enormous popularity in Scotland and England. In 1811, in the heart of the Border country near Melrose, he bought a farmhouse and spent the next twenty years turning it into the splendid Gothic pile which is Abbotsford today. It was at Abbotsford that Scott spent the last years of his life feverishly writing novels to help pay the debts left by the bankruptcy in 1825 of the Edinburgh publishing house which he had helped

establish. It was also from Abbotsford that Scott planned much of the enormously successful public relations exercise, culminating in the State Visit of George IV to Scotland in 1822, that restored Scotland's pride in itself as a nation after the disasters of the Jacobite rebellions of the 18th century.

Abbotsford, which is still lived in by the Scott family, is open to the public in the summer months. Visitors can see Scott's study, little altered from the time he used it, as well as numerous other splendidly decorated and furnished rooms, many of them containing the fascinating relics of Scottish history collected by Scott, including Rob Roy's purse, a lock of Bonnie Prince Charlie's hair and Robbie Burns' drinking glass.

Other places with strong Scott connections in the Borders are Smailholm Tower, one of the best-preserved and most interesting of the Borders' numerous peel towers, which Scott knew well

James Hogg

because it was near Sandyknowe Farm, and Dryburgh Abbey, where he is buried.

Tibbie Shiels Inn, an inn at the southern end of St Mary's Loch, in the heart of the Ettrick Forest region, can boast of connections with both Walter Scott and James Hogg, the 'Ettrick shepherd', for the two writers met here several times to talk about their work. James Hogg was born in Ettrick in 1770 and, although he had little formal education, early showed a fine empathy with the ballads and legends of the Borders, many of them heard at his mother's knee, as well as a natural talent for writing imaginative poetry. Scott published several of Hogg's ballads in his *Border Minstrelsy*, and, after early disappointments, Hogg eventually became an established figure in Edinburgh's literary world, writing both poetry and prose. His *Private Memoirs and Confessions of A Justified Sinner* was an extraordinary work, exploring the theme of the 'split personality', as Robert Louis Stevenson was to do later in *Dr Jekyll and Mr Hyde*. Hogg is buried in the graveyard at Ettrick, where there is also a monument marking his birthplace.

Some of Hogg's poetry shows a certain indebtedness to the work of Robbie Burns, which is not surprising for Burns, a decade older than Hogg, brought an entirely new and richly invigorating style to Scottish poetry. Although Burns did not live in the Border country, coming nearest to it during his years as an excise officer in Dumfries, his famous Borders tour of 1787 left a lasting memory, not least in the many inns he stayed at and the places he visited during his tour. Near Tweedsmuir, a hamlet up on the moors near the source of the Tweed, is the Crook Inn, known to Burns, Scott and Hogg, though not all at the same time, and, late in the 19th century, to John Buchan. Burns, as was his habit, wrote a poem in the Crook Inn's kitchen. Called 'Willie Wastle's Wife', it was intended to be sung to a Borders tune.

Tweedsmuir was the name chosen by John Buchan for his title when he was made a peer in 1935. Although born in Perth, Buchan spent much of his childhood in the Border country and it was this land, rather than the Highlands, which provided the background for several of his books, including *The Thirty-Nine Steps*. There is a John Buchan Centre at Broughton, further to the north, about 5 miles from Biggar. It was in this village, right on the western edge of the Border country, that Buchan grew up, remarking much later in life that he 'liked Broughton better than any place in the world'. The John Buchan Centre, housed in a former United Free Church, provides an interesting look into the world of a man who, as well as an immensely popular writer, was a Member of Parliament, a publisher and a distinguished statesman: as the 1st Baron Tweedsmuir, he was Governor General of Canada in 1935.

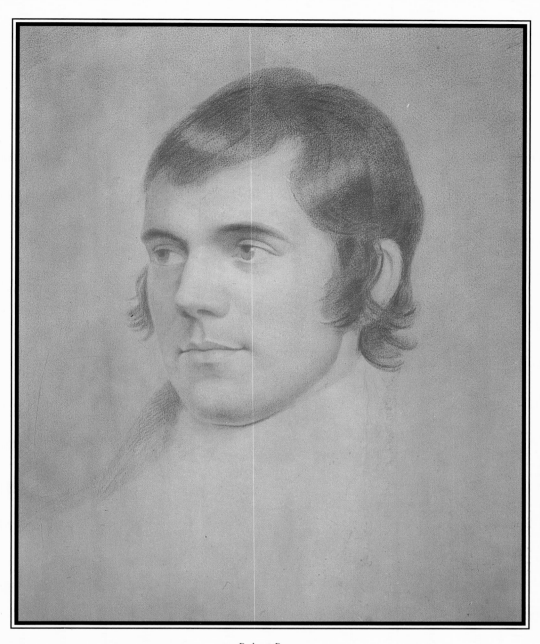

Robert Burns

OPPOSITE, TOP RIGHT
Abbotsford, Sir Walter Scott's home in the lovely country near Melrose. This splendid Gothic-style pile, still lived in by Scotts' descendants, was a simple farmhouse when Scott bought it in 1811. Both the house and its surrounding parkland owe their present-day appearance to Scott's own taste and romantic imagination. He was an enthusiastic collector of relics of Scottish history and of Scotland's great men and women, many of which are displayed in the house.

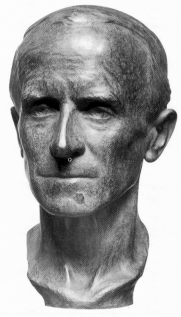

Sir John Buchan, 1st Baron Tweedsmuir

Chapter Two
Edinburgh & the Central Lowlands

ABOVE
The Palace of Holyroodhouse, official residence of the sovereign in Scotland, is set in the heart of Edinburgh.

OPPOSITE
A fortress guarding Scotland for three centuries, Tantallon Castle, built on a sheer cliff overlooking the Firth of Forth east of North Berwick, took General Monk twelve days of heavy bombardment to reduce to a ruin in 1651. Bass Rock, about one and a half miles out to sea, once had a castle, too, where Covenanters and Jacobites were imprisoned. Today, the rock is home to great colonies of seabirds.

To describe as 'lowland' this central part of Scotland, which lies on either side of the Firth of Forth roughly between the northern slopes of the Pentland Hills and Edinburgh in the south and the southern slopes of the Ochil Hills and the rolling country of Fife in the north, is to do something of an injustice to this gentle and attractive country. True, you will not find the splendid ruggedness of the north-west Highlands here, nor even the fine vistas of rolling hills cut by the waters of many rivers and lochs characteristic of the country from which the Forth flows south-east to the North Sea. What you will find is a country, more hilly than much of England, where there are green valleys and rolling, grass-clad hill country supporting much highly developed agriculture and horticulture and where, in contrast, are also to be found a large part of Scotland's industrial base, centred on places like Grangemouth on the southern shore of the Firth of Forth, and a high proportion of the country's total population.

The region's place at the northern limit of the relatively-simple-to-invade section of the map of Scotland (when looked at by English kings intent on grabbing their northern neighbour's throne for their heirs) means that in this part of Scotland you will also find many reminders of the centuries-long struggle for control of the country fought by Scots and English. At Edinburgh and Stirling are two mighty fortresses built on strategically placed hills; along the south coast of the Firth of Forth and round the headland facing the North Sea are the ruins of castles at Dirleton, Tantallon near North Berwick and Dunbar; at Dunfermline, Linlithgow and Falkland are the remains of once-favoured royal residences; and at places as far apart as Bannockburn, south of Stirling, Prestonpans, east of Edinburgh, and Dunbar are the sites of battles fought between Scots and English, rebels and government troops.

Dominating this part of Scotland is the

capital, Edinburgh. Where most of Britain's oldest cities grew along the banks of rivers and up river valleys, Edinburgh, probably starting off as an Iron Age settlement or hill fort, gradually grew along a ridge, feeling its way from the fortified building on what is now Castle Rock down to Arthur's Seat, where an abbey, called Holyrood, was founded in a forested valley early in the 12th century by that great abbey builder King David I just four years after he had moved his country's capital to Edinburgh from Dunfermline in the old Kingdom of Fife. Early in the 16th century, the abbey's guest house was taken over by James IV and developed as a royal residence.

Today, the Palace of Holyroodhouse is still the sovereign's official residence in Scotland and the ruin of the abbey, reduced to just the nave of the abbey church, is nearby in Holyrood Park. While visitors to Holyroodhouse today can see signs of the present Royal Family's residence in the later State Apartments, including a harpsichord said to be a favourite with Princess Margaret, it is to the older State Apartments that most visitors are drawn, seeking reminders of the palace's most romantic resident, Mary, Queen of Scots. Her apartments in the north-west tower are maintained as much as possible in the style she would have known. Once upon a time visitors could even see one of the blood stains which dripped from the many wounds of the queen's secretary, David Rizzio, stabbed to death outside her private parlour by a gang which included her husband, Lord Darnley; today, a discreet plaque on the floor marks the spot where Rizzio fell.

A visit to Edinburgh Castle at the other end of what is today called the Royal Mile, is, perhaps, less romantic than one to Holyroodhouse, but its military connections make it more thrilling and, for those seeking the names of relatives who died for king and country in two world wars, more moving. Edinburgh Castle's history goes much further back in time than Holyrood's, with the oldest building in the present great edifice (and, indeed, in Edinburgh) being the austerely simple Norman-style chapel built by Queen Margaret, David I's mother, towards the end of the 11th century. Also in Edinburgh Castle is the Scottish National War Memorial; the Crown Room, in which is kept the Regalia, or the Honours of Scotland, the crown, sceptre and sword of which are among the oldest royal regalia in Europe; Queen Mary's Apartments, of great significance in Scottish history because it was in a small room here that Mary, Queen of Scots gave birth to the son who would in 1603 combine the crowns of Scotland and England; and the Old Parliament Hall. The visitors' approach to Edinburgh Castle is by way of the Esplanade, site of the spectacular Military Tattoo which is a major feature of the Edinburgh Festival every year.

Old Edinburgh, the part growing along and to

either side of the route from the castle to the palace, is the Edinburgh round which the Flodden Wall was flung in the panic which followed the defeat and death of James IV at Flodden in 1513; it is the city which Henry VIII's troops devastated during the 'Rough Wooing', and it is the Edinburgh of Mary, Queen of Scots and John Knox, of Montrose and Bonnie Prince Charlie, who held court briefly in the Palace of Holyroodhouse in 1745. He never captured Edinburgh Castle, however, and his occupation of the city and palace of his Stuart ancestors was brief. King George IV had better luck. He visited Holyroodhouse during his triumphant State Visit to Scotland in 1822, stunning the guests at a state ball in the palace by dressing in full Highland regalia, complete with Royal Stewart tartan and a pair of pink tights.

Because the Flodden Wall restricted outward building, Old Edinburgh grew tall within its

confines, giving rise to the tall, multi-storied tenements or 'Lands' huddled together in wynds, closes and courts which tourists still find such a joy to explore as they wander along the Royal Mile, darting off Lawnmarket to visit Lady Stair's Close and Lady Stair's House with its relics of the great writers, Walter Scott and Robbie Burns, popping into St Giles Cathedral or visiting John Knox House off the High Street. More of Old Edinburgh may be discovered by taking Holyrood Road, which runs south of the Royal Mile back from Holyroodhouse towards Castle Mound. This road becomes Cowgate before it enters the great space of Grassmarket, once the medieval city's main cattle and hay market. The area around Grassmarket and Greyfriars Church to the south has seen a considerable amount of modern development, but still retains an atmosphere and style more in tune with the 17th and 18th centuries than the twentieth.

For a stunningly attractive 18th-century flavour, however, visitors to Edinburgh must make their way to the part of the city north of the Royal Mile which has been known since it was planned as the New Town. Edinburgh's New Town, conceived by an imaginative Lord Provost early in the 18th century, has been called one of the boldest schemes of civic architecture ever carried out in Europe. As much as the city's reputation at the time for a distinctive literary and intellectual style, the new architecture helped give 'Auld Reekie', as Edinburgh was long called because of its smoking chimneys, the much more elegant tag, 'the Athens of the North'.

The New Town, dominated by two single-sided terraces, Princes Street and Queen Street, with the fine thoroughfare of George Street between them, was laid out on land once known as Barefoot's Park on the far side of the Nor' Loch. Its fine streets and squares, with their

ABOVE
The two great bridges over the Firth of Forth near Edinburgh. On the left is the one-and-a-half-miles-long suspension bridge for road traffic, opened in 1964, and on the right is the cantilevered railway bridge, first used in 1890.

LEFT
The High Street section of the Royal Mile in Edinburgh, with John Knox House jutting out into the street at the centre of the picture. Other historic buildings along High Street range from the magnificent St Giles Cathedral (the High Kirk of Edinburgh) to one of Robbie Burns' favourite pubs, the Anchor Tavern in Anchor Close.

elegant Georgian buildings, now housing many of the institutions at the heart of Edinburgh's important financial community, and several fine churches, were completed by the end of the 18th century. Early in the 19th century came the Eastern New Town, built in the Calton Hill area of the city, the names of its main thoroughfares – Royal Terrace, Carlton Terrace, Regent Terrace, Waterloo Place – giving a clear indication of the period of their construction.

The creation of a new Edinburgh in this superbly elegant and distinctly non-fortified style was possible because the country was now at peace. Scotland and England had been united under one crown since 1603 and had been governed by one cabinet and parliament since the 1707 Act of Union. The Jacobite threat, always rumbling away in the background since James VII and II had been forced into exile in 1688, had been seen off forever at Culloden in 1746. A couple of centuries before, it had all been very different. While the kings of Scotland saw Edinburgh as the main seat of their power, they also, with a wary eye on the Border not far enough away to the south, maintained palaces and castles at a safer distance, across the Firth of Forth

and also to the west of Edinburgh in Lothian.

In Western Lothian, in the ancient town of Linlithgow, is the splendid ruin of Linlithgow Palace, where both James V and his daughter, Mary, Queen of Scots, were born. Linlithgow was granted a charter by David I and probably had a royal residence from that time. The fortified palace was built by James I and it was here that James IV's wife, Margaret, daughter of Henry VII of England was living when she heard of the death of her husband at Flodden in 1513. From the fine parish church of St Michael, next to the Palace, the bell tolled a gloomy knell for the death of the king and the flower of the Scottish nobility. While the palace, accidentally burnt down while it was occupied by the Duke of Cumberland's troops in 1746, is a roofless shell today, though with enough left to give visitors an idea of what life was like there in its great days, St Michael's Church has been carefully restored and remains one of the finest parish churches in Scotland.

In the country between Linlithgow and Edinburgh to the east lie many fine houses and castles. Prominently set on the Firth of Forth is Blackness Castle, once of such great strategic importance that the 1707 Articles of Union

specified that it should remain fortified, and, close by, the House of the Binns, maintained by the National Trust for Scotland. The superb 18th-century mansion, Hopetoun House, seat of the marquises of Linlithgow, also stands on the shores of the Forth near here. The main part of the house was the work of Scotland's finest family of architects, the Adams. William Adam and his son John were involved in the creation of Hopetoun House over a period of 50 years, creating a superbly designed setting for fine works of art, including paintings by Rembrandt, Rubens and Titian, and furniture by Thomas Chippendale.

South of Hopetoun House is Kirkliston, where Robert Adam, William Adam's other son, designed the smaller, but still elegant Newliston House. A couple of miles away is Niddry Castle, which gave shelter to Mary, Queen of Scots when she escaped from imprisonment in Loch Leven Castle in 1568.

There is also a strong royal connection at Queensferry, a few miles to the east, for this was the site of the ferry which took travellers across the Firth of Forth for 800 years until it was replaced by the two great bridges which now span the Forth upriver from the ferry site. The Forth

ABOVE
The elegant facade of Hopetoun House, reflected in the still waters of the lake which is a feature of the parkland surrounding the house.

LEFT
There has been a fortification on the site of Edinburgh Castle since the time of the Picts.

ABOVE
Dunfermline Abbey, in whose church are buried many of Scotland's kings and queens, including Queen Margaret and Robert the Bruce.

LEFT
Linlithgow Palace, birthplace of James V and his daughter Mary, Queen of Scots.

BELOW
The 'Royal and Ancient' Golf Club at St Andrews. Of the four courses at St Andrews, the famous Old Course is the oldest in the world.

railway bridge was opened in 1890 and the magnificent suspension bridge for road traffic in 1964. Queensferry took its name from Queen Margaret (canonized in 1251) who used the ferry many times to get to and from her favourite palace at Dunfermline, on the north shore of the Firth in the Kingdom of Fife.

Queen Margaret and her husband, Malcolm III, built a palace and a priory at Dunfermline. The palace was occupied by a succession of Scotland's rulers and even, for a time, by Edward I of England, right down to the 17th century, when Charles II lived there before marching down to England and defeat at Worcester. Charles' father, Charles I and his sister Elizabeth were both born at Dunfermline. Little remains of the palace that is identifiable, apart from a kitchen, but the great abbey church still stands proudly nearby, sheltering within its walls the remains of Malcolm's and Margaret's sons Edgar, Alexander I and David I and their descendants Malcolm IV,

Alexander III and Robert the Bruce (but not the Bruce's heart; it is said to have been taken on a crusade before being brought back to Scotland for burial in Melrose Abbey).

Today, Fife is one of Scotland's local government regions, covering a peninsula of land between the firths of the Forth and the Tay rivers. For many centuries, its geographical position tended to keep the Kingdom of Fife, so-called because Dunfermline had been the home of Scotland's kings from the 11th century, somewhat isolated from the main stream of Scottish affairs. In our own time, the opening of two road bridges, the Forth in 1964 and the Tay in 1966, has changed things noticeably. Visitors have been coming in increasing numbers to this country with its fine coastal scenery, attractive holiday resorts and famous golf courses.

Much of Fife is farming country, especially along the agriculturally rich valley of the Howe of Fife, lying at the foot of the Lomond Hills, with stretches of moorland over the higher country. From the holidaymaker's point of view, Fife's most attractive country is the length of coastline at the eastern end of its southern coast called the East Neuk, which runs roughly between Elie and Crail, south of Fife Ness. Along here is a string of picturesque old fishing towns which have also become pleasant resorts and artists' colonies.

The main city of Fife is St Andrews, built round St Andrews Bay at the eastern edge of the peninsula. St Andrews can boast of possessing the oldest university in Scotland, founded in 1410, and the world's oldest golf course, the famous Old Course, scene of many a thrilling British Open. Although golf has been played at St Andrews for at least 500 years, its famous Royal and Ancient Golf Club dates from only 1754.

St Andrews' early history was largely church-oriented, so that by the beginning of the 10th century, the bishopric of St Andrews was the prime one in Scotland. The 15th and 16th centuries saw a good deal of religious strife in St Andrews, culminating in the burning of a Protestant, George Wishart, at the order of the Roman Catholic Cardinal Beaton in 1546, a deed which was pretty soon avenged by the murder of the Cardinal. By this time, Scottish royalty had begun to make its presence felt in St Andrews, Mary of Guise being welcomed to Scotland with much ceremony in the town on the occasion of her marriage to James V in 1538.

Although their daughter, Mary, Queen of Scots visited St Andrews twice, her longest stay in the Kingdom of Fife was not a happy one. After her hasty marriage to James, Earl of Bothwell in 1567 led to her downfall, Mary was imprisoned on a castle in the middle of Loch Leven, at the western end of Fife. She was there nearly a year before managing to make her escape. Today, Loch Leven attracts many visitors because of the quality

of its fishing, though in the attractive little town of Kinross on the loch's shore visitors intent on tracing the main events in the Queen's ultimately tragic life can arrange summertime boat trips to the castle in the loch.

A few miles north-east of Loch Leven is the picturesque little town of Falkland, where Falkland Palace, now in the care of the National Trust for Scotland, was a favourite royal residence and hunting lodge until James VI's death in 1625.

Although Charles II stayed at Falkland Palace for a time after his father's execution, the palace was later allowed to fall into ruin. It was rescued late in the 19th century by the third Marquis of Bute, who restored it to all its early Renaissance glory, complete with beautiful gardens and the oldest tennis court in Scotland, built for James V in 1539.

Quite different from the palaces of Fife was Stirling, the great castle and royal residence which

PAGES 28-29
Snow blankets Dumgoyne, a hamlet in Strath Blane, at the western edge of the Campsie Fells.

OPPOSITE, TOP
Crail, an old fishing village on Fife's East Neuk coast, is today an attractive holiday town.

OPPOSITE, BOTTOM
The university city of St Andrews in Fife, seen from the tower of St Rule's Church, built in about 1130. The ruins in the foreground are of the cathedral, which was founded not long after the church. It fell into ruin after the Reformation.

ABOVE
Mary, Queen of Scots was imprisoned in Loch Leven Castle, on an island in Loch Leven, for nearly a year before managing to escape in 1568. Today, the loch is as famous for its fishing as for the romantic story of its royal captive.

LEFT
This view of Stirling is from Abbey Craig, from where Scotland's hero, William Wallace, worked out how he would defeat the English at the Battle of Stirling Bridge in 1297.

OVERLEAF
The Lomond Hills in Fife.

still dominates the third area of this lowland region, though it has not been a royal residence since James VI went south to became king of England. The massive bulk of Stirling Castle stands high on a volcanic plug above the Forth, dominating the plain, or Carse, surrounding it. Its position, guarding the ways to Perth and the Highlands over the lowest bridgeable point on the Forth, made the castle of great strategic importance for centuries. In English hands in 1297, it was recaptured for Scotland by William Wallace at the Battle of Stirling Bridge, only to fall back into English hands a century later.

The castle, which by the end of the 18th century had fallen into such a state of disrepair and neglect that Robbie Burns was moved to comment on it in several scathing lines of verse in 1787, has been carefully restored to its former splendour, as befits a castle in which James II was born and in which Mary, Queen of Scots was crowned at the age of nine months.

The view south from Stirling Castle is towards Bannockburn, three miles away, where, in 1314, Robert the Bruce routed the greatly superior forces of Edward II of England, taking back Stirling Castle from the English who had held it for ten years and securing Scotland's independence from then on. The 58-acre battlefield site, despite being on relatively uninteresting land edged by modern housing estates, is now a major tourist attraction where the National Trust for Scotland has provided excellent displays detailing the course of the battle. The heroic statue of Bruce on his horse, set where his command post during the battle is thought to have been, is a modern one and was unveiled by the Queen in 1964.

William Wallace's heroic life, including his earlier victory at Stirling Bridge, and his successes in clearing the English out of Perth and Lanark, as well as his execution in 1305, are also remembered by a monument. This is the Wallace Monument at Abbey Craig near Bridge of Allan, a village whose rural charms so pleased Robbie Burns, after his disappointment at Stirling, that he was inspired there to write one of his best-known songs, 'The Banks of Allan Water'.

Bridge of Allan became a popular spa in the 19th century, which perhaps helps explain why the Wallace Monument, built in 1870, is in such an over-ornate Victorian style. It is worth visiting, not just for having on display what is said to be the great patriot's two-handed sword, but for the views from the top of the tower of the Scotland over which Scots and English fought for so long. To the north are the southern slopes of the Ochil Hills, with Perth away to the north beyond, and to the south the land stretches away to the Firth of Forth where it is sometimes possible to see the flare-stacks of the petrochemical works at Grangemouth.

Scotland's Kings and Queens

The earliest people to settle in Scotland had no rulers. They were migrants from the Mediterranean region or from the western seaboard of Europe, first appearing about 3000 BC. By the time the Romans reached Scotland, about 80 years after the birth of Christ, the country was populated by tribes from many parts of Europe.

The Romans penetrated far less into Scotland's life than they did in England, leaving no fine network of roads or long strings of forts round which markets might grow up. By the time they retreated in AD 185, not much more remained to mark their passage than a few Lowland forts and the wall which the Emperor Antoninus Pius had ordered to be built between the firths of the Clyde and the Forth rivers.

The fourth century AD saw more invasions of Britain by Picts, Scots, Saxons and Franks and the coming of Christianity to Scotland, St Ninian founding a church at Whithorn in 397. Gradually, the various tribes in mainland Scotland came together into four kingdoms. In the north were the

Picts, a red-haired people who may have been a mixture of Celts and an earlier people. In the west, around present-day Argyll, were the Scots, Gaelic-speaking Christians who had come from Ireland with St Columba in the 6th century; they called their kingdom Dalriada. Also in the west and south were Britons, mostly from Wales. In the south and east were the same Germanic Angles who had moved into northern England; their kingdom was called Bernicia, or Lothian. Round about the 8th century, Norsemen from Scandinavia moved into the Hebrides, Orkney and Shetland.

While the Norsemen remained in the Hebrides until the 13th century and, in name at least, in Orkney and Shetland until the 15th century, on the mainland the kingdoms began to merge. First, in the 9th century, the Picts and Scots united under Kenneth I (Kenneth Macalpine), with the new kingdom being called first Alba, then Scotia. When Malcolm II of Scotia joined his kingdom with Lothian in the 11th century, he became the first king of a largely

united mainland Scotland.

Malcolm II's grandson, Duncan, who reigned from 1034 to 1040, completed the unification of the Scottish kingdoms when he inherited Strathclyde. As William Shakespeare has ensured we all know, Duncan was murdered by Macbeth; contrary to what Shakespeare would have us believe, however, Macbeth ruled Scotland quietly and well for 17 years before he was murdered in turn by Malcolm III, called Malcolm Canmore (meaning 'Big Head').

Malcolm's consort was an English princess, the saintly Queen Margaret, whose influence on Scotland's religious and political life was profound. The three sons of Malcolm and Margaret who ruled Scotland in succession were all pious Christians, in an English rather than Celtic style, were all English-speaking and all ruled very much in the style of the Normans in England. Although the anglicization of the Scottish court and the Scottish Lowlands had begun, relations between Scotland and her southern neighbour became increasingly difficult,

James II

Just six when his father was murdered in 1436, James II's early years as king were marked by feuding between Scotland's nobles and the boy's mother for control over him. Once he gained power he ruled wisely and well. He was killed in 1460, besieging Roxburgh Castle.

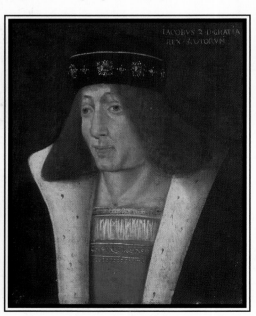

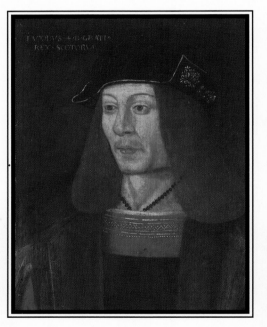

James IV

As with James II, the murder of his father brought James IV to the throne while still a boy. As ruler, he proved effective but was unable to avoid quarrels with the English, despite his English wife, a daughter of Henry VII. His death at Flodden in 1513 was a tragedy for Scotland.

Mary of Guise

A daughter of the Guises, dukes of Lorraine, Mary of Guise became Regent of Scotland in 1554, her husband, James V, having died in 1542, when their daughter Mary was less than a year old. Her dependence on French support roused Scotland's Protestant nobles to rebellion which continued into her daughter's reign.

partly because of disputed claims to the feudal overlordship of lands on both sides of the border.

The last king to rule Scotland in direct line from Malcolm III was Alexander III, during whose long reign in the 12th century Scotland knew a period of prosperity and political stability. When Alexander III died in 1286, his heir was his infant granddaughter, Margaret, the 'Maid of Norway'. In the wings, as it were, were another dozen or so claimants to the throne, including John Balliol and Robert the Bruce. In England, Edward I saw a golden opportunity. He agreed to guarantee Margaret's succession to the throne of Scotland in return for her betrothal to his son, Edward. Unfortunately, Margaret died on her way home to Scotland from Norway in 1290 and the opportunity to unite the crowns of Scotland and England without war or bloodshed was lost. Edward I of England's attempt to force himself on Scotland as the country's feudal overlord, appointing John Balliol his vassal king, led to a period of Scottish resistance which ended in success for Scotland in battle at Bannockburn in 1314 and then in the political Declaration of Arbroath in 1320, though it was some time before the English crown finally gave up its claims to Scotland. The victor at Bannockburn, Robert the Bruce, was confirmed in his position as king of Scotland.

But Robert the Bruce's son, David II, was a weak king and a period of struggle between the crown and various powerful families, some of whom called on the English king for support, now descended on Scotland. The first of the Stewarts to mount the throne, in 1371, was David II's nephew, Robert, son of Robert the Bruce's daughter Marjorie Bruce and Walter the Steward. Under the Stewarts, who changed the spelling of their name to 'Stuart' during Mary, Queen of Scots' reign, the Orkney and Shetland islands were integrated into Scotland after the marriage of James III to Margaret, the daughter of Christian I of Norway and Denmark in 1468; apparently Christian could not afford to pay his daughter's dowry, so pledged the islands instead.

The Stuart period in Scotland was not without turmoil, because so many of the Stuart kings died or were killed while still young, leaving as their heirs infants over whom rival powerful families tried to assert their authority. James I was assassinated at Perth, James II was killed by an exploding cannon while besieging Roxburgh Castle; James IV was killed at Flodden, pursuing a pro-French and anti-English policy; and James V also died young after another defeat at the hands of the English at Solway Moss in 1542. His heir, his daughter Mary, was just nine months old when she was crowned Queen in Stirling Castle. A belligerent attempt by Henry VIII to marry his son Edward to Mary caused the Scots to turn to France for support and five-year-old Mary was sent to France, where she was given a classical education, and where she married the Dauphin of France in 1558.

James V's prophecy, expressed on his death bed, that the Stuart line, which had begun with a woman (Marjorie Bruce) would also end with one, was not fulfilled. Despite proving herself quite unsuited to the task of ruling Scotland, Mary, Queen of Scots was forced to abdicate in favour, not of some suitable, preferably Protestant, Scottish lord, but of her infant son, James. This Stuart, the sixth to be called James, turned out to be both long-lived and capable of siring healthy children. There is still Stuart blood to be traced in the present royal family: when George of Hanover became King George I in 1714 on the death of Queen Anne, the last of the House of Stuart, it was because he was a direct Protestant descendant of James VI and I, through James' daughter, Elizabeth of Bohemia.

Mary, Queen of Scots

Scotland's most romantic queen, Mary, Queen of Scots ruled Scotland for less than six years before she was forced to abdicate in favour of her son, who became James VI. Seen as a Catholic threat to the Protestant English throne, Mary spent many years imprisoned in England before being executed in 1587.

James VI and I

A weak man who ruled through favourites, James VI's mixture of well-read scholarship and political foolishness earned him the tag of 'wisest fool in Christendom'. Under him, the thrones of Scotland and England were finally united.

George IV

The first of the Hanoverian kings to make anything of his Scottish blood, however diluted, George IV's State Visit to Scotland in 1822 set the seal on the revival of Scotland's cultural life after the low point of the defeat of the Jacobite cause at Culloden.

Chapter Three
The Highlands: the North-East

The great triangle of land with its apex jutting out into the North Sea which makes up the north-east part of Scotland is a country of wonderful variety. There is fine hill and mountain scenery dominated by the Grampians and the Cairngorms; there are lovely vistas of rolling hill country providing rich agricultural land in the northern counties of Banff, Moray and Buchan and in Aberdeenshire, Perthshire and Angus; and there are beautiful straths, glens and valleys watered by many burns and rivers, including the Dee, the Don and the Spey in the north-east and the rivers of the Tay basin to the west, the quality of the fishing in which attract anglers from all over the world. The quality of the river water itself has for centuries provided the basis for some of Scotland's most famous whisky brands, both malts and blended; in Perth are distilleries whose products carry the labels of some of the world's best-selling whiskies, while the distilleries of the Spey valley are so famous a Malt Whisky Trail has been devised to guide visitors around a selection of them.

This part of Scotland is also blessed with many of the country's most beautiful lochs, celebrated in song and poetry. Loch Earn, west of Perth, is one of the most popular with Scottish holidaymakers, for it is within easy driving distance through attractive countryside of Glasgow, Edinburgh and Stirling. Further north, the glorious long and narrow Loch Tay, a classic 'ribbon loch' famous for its salmon fishing, is set in an attractive countryside of small farms, dotted with woodland and, in fine contrast, the ruins of castles, mills and stone circles, attesting to a long history of settlement. Further north again comes the chain of lochs and streams dominated by lochs Rannoch and Tummel.

In these valleys and in the rolling hill country of the whole region are many superb examples of that uniquely Scottish style of architecture, the tower house, or keep, rising out of finely kept estate lands to dominate the country around them. Most perfectly preserved of them is Craigievar Castle, nestling in the foothills of the Grampians west of Aberdeen. The castle was built early in the 17th century for a rich merchant called William Forbes, whose trade in the Baltic had earned him the nickname of Danzig Willie, and has been left virtually unchanged since its construction. Then there is Braemar, in the Dee valley, a real fortress tower, and, much further north near Nairn, Cawdor. The original Cawdor may have been the

castle where Macbeth murdered Duncan and although the present castle dates from several centuries after Macbeth, it still has at its heart a strong, typically Scottish fortress tower.

Other historic castles of the region may have lost their typical tower shape during rebuilding over the centuries, but the tower is usually still to be found somewhere at the heart of the later building. Glamis Castle, for instance, near Forfar in Angus and the historic home of the Bowes-Lyon family, whose head is the Earl of Strathmore and Kinghorne and whose most famous member is Her Majesty Queen Elizabeth the Queen Mother, may look a wonderfully theatrical pile of turrets and battlements, but it is built round an ancient square tower with walls many feet thick. Scone Palace, near Perth, was rebuilt early in the

RIGHT
There is some dispute about why this famous view of lovely Loch Tummel is called Queen's View; it is certain that Queen Victoria, coming here in 1886, was much impressed by the view over the loch towards Schiehallion, but some people think that the name may have been given to the view long before then, perhaps even as far back as Mary, Queen of Scots' reign.

BELOW
Fairy-tale Craigievar Castle, a mass of conical roofs and turrets, has been continuously occupied since it was built early in the 17th century near the market town of Alford on the Don river.

19th century by its owner, the Earl of Mansfield, but even here there are enough remains of the much older building to alert the visitor to the centuries-long history of this important site.

A glance at the map shows that for administrative purposes the north-east of Scotland comprises just two local government regions, Tayside, which includes Perthshire and Angus, in the south and Grampian in the north. In this chapter, we are going to travel beyond the western edges of the local government borders into the southern section of the Highland region, below the Great Glen, a more geographically satisfying demarcation line between north-east and north-west Scotland.

The eastern and northern borders of this region are North Sea-facing coasts, along which, encountered as you come up from the south, are historic towns such as Arbroath, Montrose and Stonehaven; Scotland's third largest city and Europe's 'oil capital', Aberdeen; the important fishing ports of Peterhead and Fraserburgh; and, round the apex of the triangle, the ancient towns of Banff, Elgin and Nairn. As in the triangle of Fife to the south, two rivers and their firths, those of the Tay and the Moray, mark the south and north borders of the region.

Two historic towns, Perth and Dundee, lie beside 'the silv'ry Tay', to quote Scotland's

favourite bad poet, William McGonagall. Dundee is in Angus, on the north shore of the Firth of Tay, at the point where the Firth narrows sufficiently to be bridged by both rail and road bridges. The collapse in December 1879 of the first rail bridge, taking nearly a hundred train passengers to their deaths in the icy waters below, inspired McGonagall's most famous doggerel:

'... Then the central girders with a crash gave way.
And down went the train and passengers into the Tay!
The storm fiend did loudly bray,
Because ninety lives had been taken away,
On the last Sabbath day of 1879,
Which will be remember'd for a very long time.'

Perth is further inland, at the heart of Perthshire, an area of long-established moorland sporting estates, exclusive golf courses like Gleneagles and rich farming country set in a fine landscape of lovely wooded glens and quiet lochs. While both Perth and Dundee are both ancient royal burghs which have played significant parts in Scotland's political and economic history, Perth is, perhaps, the more interesting town to visit, partly because much of the ancient centre of Dundee was demolished in the 19th century, and a lot of post-war building there has been of the dreary concrete slab variety.

as a main setting for his eponymous novel, it is also important as a base from which to explore some of Scotland's loveliest countryside. To the west, beyond the attractive town of Crieff, for centuries an important 'tryst', or cattle market, lie Loch Earn and the Sma' Glen. A main road north-east, the A93, is the road to Aberdeen, taking the traveller via Blairgowrie and Glen Shee, where the Spittal of Glenshee can provide interesting skiing when the snow has been right, to Braemar and Royal Deeside.

The main road north from Perth is the A9, one of Scotland's major roads. Its great attraction for the visitor is the fact that as it curves north-east from Perth, via the historic towns of Dunkeld, Pitlochry and Blair Atholl to Dalwhinnie, the A9 encloses to the west an exceptionally fine area of typically Scottish loch and glen scenery. This is the area of the Tay basin, Scotland's watershed, where the glaciation of the last Ice Age left a

Perth's roots reach far back into history. If the town's rectangular street pattern is anything to go by, the Romans may have built a camp at this point on the Tay which, so legend has it, they likened to the Tiber when they first saw it. In the 9th century, Kenneth Macalpine made Scone, two miles north of present-day Perth, the capital of his kingdom of Alba.

In medieval times, Perth grew in importance as a civil and religious centre: at one time the town contained monasteries belonging to four different religious orders, the White Friars, the Black Friars, the Grey Friars and the Carthusians, all of which were destroyed during the uprising which followed John Knox's fiery preaching against idolatory in Perth's St John's Church in 1559.

Its position at the heart of central Scotland meant that Perth, like Dundee, was the focus of much unwelcome military action. The town was occupied by Edward I, the 'hammer of the Scots', taken by Robert the Bruce, re-taken by the English, then wrested back by the Scots.... This pattern was repeated in the 17th century in the times of Cromwell and Montrose, then again in the 18th century, during the Jacobite rebellions. By this time, Perth was an important town and port in central Scotland, and had been exporting wool and whisky, still one of the town's major businesses, since the 16th century. It was also, during the period of the Franco-Scottish 'Auld Alliance', a great importer of claret from Bordeaux.

While Perth today is a major business and agricultural centre and a handsome town, with many historic buildings to interest the visitor, including St John's Church, 15th-century Balhousie Castle, which houses the Black Watch Museum, and the Fair Maid of Perth's House, the former Glovers' Hall chosen by Sir Walter Scott

myriad of corries in the high mountains to provide the rock basins for some seventy major lochs and countless lochans, which drain into the river systems of four great rivers, the Garry, Tummel, Earn and Tay. Extensive hydro-electric work, including dam building, in this area has created even more lochs, such as Loch Errochty in the north, and greatly increased the size of others, including Loch Tummel.

Here is a country of heather moors, of the wild and bleak isolation of Rannoch Moor and Glen Coe in the far west, of forests and glens, some of them open and some enclosed by great walls of rocks down which rivers and waterfalls tumble. The Pass of Killiecrankie, on the A9 between Bridge of Garry and Blair Atholl, where the River Garry forces its way through a narrow wooded gorge to join the Tummel, is perhaps the best-known and certainly the most romantic of the area's river gorges. Here in 1689, English forces

of William III were defeated by a band of Jacobite Highlanders led by John Graham of Claverhouse, Viscount Dundee. 'Bonnie Dundee', as the ballads call him, was killed in the battle. Robert Burns and Queen Victoria can be counted among the many thousands of people who have paused here to stand before the stone marking the place where Bonnie Dundee fell wounded.

While this area includes several of the most-visited lochs in Scotland, including lochs Rannoch, Tummel, Tay and Earn, it also has many hidden so deep in glens and forests which are bird-watchers' paradises that they are accessible only to walkers and backpackers. No wonder that Bonnie Prince Charlie and his small band of followers chose to build a hideout among holly trees near a cave, called Cluny's Cave, above remote Loch Ericht, set in high moorland surrounded by mountains, to be his last refuge before he escaped to France in 1746.

After the Pass of Killiecrankie, the A9 takes the traveller easily through Blair Atholl, where the Duke of Atholl, comfortably ensconced in stylish Blair Castle, is the only private citizen in Britain allowed to maintain an army, the Atholl Highlanders. Then the road winds through Glen Garry and up through the Grampian mountains via the barren Pass of Drummochter past Dalwhinnie at the northern end of Loch Ericht and so into the eastern edge of the Highlands region. It passes through Newtonmore and Kingussie, where the bleak ruins of Ruthven Barracks are a reminder of the oppressive treatment meted out to the Highlands after the 1715 Jacobite uprising, and so between the Monadhliath mountains in the west and the Cairngorms in the east, before reaching Aviemore, Britain's best-organized winter sports town.

Since it was very much a creation of the 1960s, when grey concrete was too much the order of the day for Britain's architects and townplanners, Aviemore is not a particularly attractive town but it does have all the right amenities to make it an excellent base for snow and ice sports in winter and for some fine walking, backpacking and pony trekking in the Cairngorms and the Glenmore Forest Park in summer.

At Aviemore the A9 turns away from the valley of the River Spey, which it has been following since Newtonmore, to head towards Inverness at the top of the Great Glen. The Spey rises in the Monadhliath mountains and flows north-east across the wildlife-rich wood and farmland of Strathspey to flow into the Moray Firth east of Elgin and Lossiemouth.

Among places of historic interest in this area is Elgin, the administrative centre of Moray. Elgin's 12th-century cathedral, now a picturesque ruin, was once dubbed 'the lantern of the north' – until the notorious Alexander Stewart, the Wolf of Badenoch, who was an outlawed son of Robert II, set fire to it. Near Elgin are Gordonstoun School, where all three of the Queen's sons were educated, following in the footsteps of their father, Prince Philip, and, 9 km (6 miles) to the southwest, Pluscarden Abbey, where a new generation of Benedictine monks is rebuilding and restoring the abbey founded by Alexander II in the early 13th century.

There is no denying, however, that of greater interest than abbeys or schools to most of the Spey valley's visitors are the superb salmon fishing in the Spey and whisky – especially the latter. Whisky distilling has been an important activity in the area for so long that Speyside malts are one of the great classifications of Scotch whisky. The whisky distilling area reaches from Grantown-on-Spey all the way to the coast, with so many distilleries operating that a typical sight of the area is plumes of white steam rising up into the sky from distilleries which would otherwise be

hidden from view among the trees and hills. One of the best places to visit to find out all you need to know about whisky distilling is the Glenfiddich distillery at Dufftown. Many of the other famous names of the Speyside malt whisky business also have visitor centres, and there is a Malt Whisky Trail, leaflets about which are available at the tourist information centres of the area, as well as at the distilleries themselves. Walkers on the Speyside Way, which runs 75 km (45 miles) from Spey Bay on the coast to Tomintoul, find that their path also passes several distilleries.

Tomintoul, the highest village in the Highlands, was laid out in 1779 by the Duke of Gordon, one of the leading Scots statesmen of the day and a patron of Robert Burns. Here, on this bleak moorland, we can see how the somewhat distant rule of the Stuarts kings and queens of Scotland was superseded by the more practical ruthlessness of the Hanoverians. The A939, which winds its way across the moorland south of Tomintoul to Deeside, follows for part of its way the notoriously steep Lecht Road, often the first road in Scotland to be closed when winter snows strike. This fine piece of road building was achieved by several companies of the 33rd Regiment of the British Army in the years immediately after the 1745 rebellion. In building the road they were carrying on the work begun by the English General George Wade after 1715; his network of metalled roads and 40 fine stone bridges was a wonderfully tactful way of pacifying the Highland clans and bringing them

into the fold of Great Britain. While the Lecht Road was being built, the government also took over 16th-century Corgarff Castle, at the road's southern end, and turned it into a bleak-looking military barracks; once the Jacobite threat was past, the barracks formed a useful military base from which the government could suppress smuggling, especially of whisky.

The barracks was still used by the military until just a few years before Queen Victoria ascended the throne. The last of the Hanoverians, Victoria was also the first of the post-Stuart sovereigns to develop a love for the Scottish Highlands that remains undiminished in today's Royal Family. In 1852, Victoria and her husband, Prince Albert, bought an estate called Balmoral on the Dee, in a beautiful country of moorland, forest and hill dominated by 1164m (3786ft) Lochnagar rising to the south. With the help of Aberdeen's city architect, they replaced the old tower castle there with a castle in a Victorian baronial style which was copied on so many Scottish estates that it came to be almost as uniquely Scottish an architectural style as the much older tower house. (Many of these Scottish baronial piles are now comfortable country house hotels, adding greatly to the pleasure of touring in Scotland.) In fact, Victoria and Albert started many fashions still followed by well-to-do Scots and English people in Scotland, including late summer shooting parties on grouse moors, attending Highland Games (at Braemar for those living at Balmoral), whisky drinking, tartan carpets, servants in kilts

and Scottish country dancing.

Although the gardens of Balmoral Castle are open only when the Royal Family is not in residence, while just a couple of rooms in the castle itself are shown to the public, the very presence of royalty has helped turn Deeside into one of Scotland's major tourist attractions. Even without Balmoral Castle, there is plenty to interest the visitor to this beautiful part of the Highlands. Near Balmoral itself is Crathie Church, where the Royal Family worship when they are in Scotland, and where the Princess Royal married her second husband, Commander Timothy Laurence. The Royal Lochnagar Distillery, which produced Queen Victoria's favourite dram, has a visitor centre and offers tours of the distillery.

Braemar, 14 km (9 miles) west of Balmoral, is famous both for its round-towered castle and for the Highland Games held there every September. Nearby, at the beauty spot called Linn o' Dee, river waters cascade into a series of rocky pools. In the surrounding Forest of Mar is much fine walking country, taking in the foothills of 131lm (4296ft) Ben Macdhui.

East of Balmoral, the A93, the main road to Aberdeen, follows the bank of the rock-strewn River Dee, a favourite fishing stretch for the Royal Family, passing several interesting towns, including Ballater, built at the end of the 18th century to bring visitors to the nearby spa of Pannanich Wells, and Aboyne, famous for its Highland Gathering each September.

At Banchory, where the Water of Feugh joins

The great peak of Lochnagar, 1164 metres (3786 feet) high, seen from Blacksheil Burn on Royal Deeside. The mountain dominates the horizon south of the royal estate at Balmoral and inspired Prince Charles' first book, The Old Man of Lochnagar, *written to amuse his young brothers.*

The wild beauty and remoteness of Glen Coe would have made it a romantic place, even without its turbulent history. The infamous massacre of the Macdonalds of Glen Coe by a troop of soldiers led by Campbell of Glenlyon in 1692, ostensibly because they had not sworn allegiance to King William III, is remembered as one of the darkest deeds of treachery in Scottish history. Today, Glen Coe can still be a dangerous place, especially for walkers and climbers caught unprepared for the rapidly changing weather conditions for which the area is notorious.

the Dee, several roads go north towards the valley of the Don into a country dotted with castles, including Castle Fraser, a massive building in the care of the National Trust for Scotland near Kemnay and Craigievar, to the north-west. The maps of the area also indicate numerous prehistoric sites, a reminder that fifty per cent of Scotland's standing stones, as well as other prehistoric remains, are to be found in the Grampian region.

Past Banchory, the A93, still following the Dee, passes Crathes Castle, one of the finest Jacobean houses in Scotland and well worth visiting, especially for its wonderfully decorative ceilings in rooms with such romantic names as the Room of the Nine Nobles and the Room of the Green Lady, a ghost said to walk, with her baby, through several rooms in the castle.

Another 10km (6 miles) down the glen is Drum Castle (NTS), where a crow-stepped gabled mansion was added to the original thick-walled medieval keep early in the 17th century. A few miles' drive from Drum brings the traveller to the outskirts of Aberdeen, Scotland's third largest city.

There is a belief current that Aberdeen, the 'Granite City' which all Scotsmen either love or loathe, has been utterly transformed by the discovery of oil in the North Sea. It is true that the city's airport and harbour, in particular, have been greatly enlarged to cope with the air and sea traffic of the oil fields and that there has been a great deal of office, hotel and conference centre building. But

Aberdeen, built on and built out of granite, has been a self-confident, solidly-based city for generations and still retains the rather dour self-confidence it has known since its industrialization at the beginning of the 19th century.

The city of Aberdeen falls into two parts. Old Aberdeen, an area of cobbled streets and houses, many of them dating from the 16th century, has the city's oldest cathedral, St Machar's, and King's College, the oldest part of the university, within its bounds. Central Aberdeen, with its more formal rows of granite-built houses and terraces, is where most of the city's art galleries, museums, markets, and university buildings are to be found, dotted around the two main thoroughfares of Broad Street and Union Street. Down in the harbour area, off Market Street, is Aberdeen's Maritime Museum and its splendidly modern Fish Market, the biggest in Scotland, and a reminder that fish have been sold and auctioned in Aberdeen for at least seven centuries.

Although approaching Aberdeen from the west tends to give the visitor the feeling that Aberdeen is in a somewhat isolated position, set on the edge of the North Sea between the arms of two rivers, the Don and the Dee, it is, in fact, not much more than a fifty-mile drive down to Dundee on the Firth of Tay. The city is also the gateway to some of Scotland's most unspoilt coastline to the north. Up to Cruden Bay and on to the busy Buchan fishing ports of Peterhead, Western Europe's biggest whitefish port, and Fraserburgh stretch many miles of unspoilt beaches.

Scotland and Whisky

Whisky was probably first distilled in Scotland in the 15th century, largely for medicinal purposes. Historians guess that Scotsmen were first alerted to the properties of distilled alcohol by the Irish, who had been making 'aqua vitae' (or 'water of life', the Gaelic for which is 'uisge beatha') since the 12th century.

Scotland, with a climate too cold for growing grapes, proved to be ideally suited to the production of distilled alcohol based on grains such as barley. There was plenty of high quality water, essential for the distillation process, and there were abundant supplies of peat to provide the fuel which gives whisky its unique flavour and taste – or flavours and tastes, for it is the great diversity of both which gives whisky its unique place among the distilled alcohols of the world.

For centuries, whisky distilling was a home-based business, with farmers and local lairds producing just enough for family use. It took on a greater importance in national life when Scotland's 'Auld Alliance' with France, during which the trade in wine between the two countries

had been considerable, came to an abrupt end with the alliance of the crowns of Scotland and England. In time, of course, the government came to see the value of whisky as a revenue earner and its production and trade came to be regularized by various acts of parliament. Occasionally, in times of poor harvests, the business even had to be strictly limited, so as to preserve the country's grain crops for food. Despite this, by the end of the 18th century the whisky distilling industry was part of the fabric of Scottish life – as was the business of avoiding excise duty on it. During the 19th century whisky grew into one of the country's biggest export earners.

Whisky production is a long-drawn-out process, involving soaking the grain, then putting it through processsess of germination, or 'malting', fermentation, distillation and maturation. It is during the last process, which is done in wooden casks, that a malt whisky takes on its unique character and colour. Unlike wine, whisky does not mature in the bottle, so the best malt whiskies are likely to have spent from eight to fifteen or twenty years in the cask.

The Scotch whisky industry is based on two types: single malt whisky, which is made from malted barley, and grain whisky, which is made from maize and a certain amount of malted barley. Blended whiskies, which are blends of the two types with grain whisky predominating but with their distinctive flavours coming from the malt whiskies used in the blending, account for more than 90 per cent of all whisky sales. To make sure there is a whisky to suit every taste, the distillers and blenders have come up with various special blends, such as de luxe whiskies, which are blends of aged malts and well-matured grain whiskies and vatted malts, which are blends of malt whiskies only.

Malt whiskies are classified in four groups, depending on their geographical origins: Highland, Lowland, Campbeltown and Islay. Connoisseurs can tell which area a single malt comes from by its flavour. Highland malts are the most numerous and include the great Speyside malts; Islay and Campbeltown malts have strong, peaty flavours and Lowland malts are softer and lighter in flavour than the others and tend to be used as a cushion between the heavier malts and the grain whiskies used in the blend.

For the novice whisky drinker wanting to become more expert, there is no better place in Scotland to go to than Speyside, in the north-east. Here is the so-called 'Golden Triangle' of the whisky business, centred on Dufftown and containing rivers like the Livet and the Spey, the purity and abundance of the waters of which is vital to the production of fine malt whisky. The fact that the Spey is also one of Scotland's finest salmon fishing rivers gives the area a double attraction.

Speyside's Malt Whisky Trail is a well-planned and mapped 70-mile route taking in some eight distilleries which offer guided tours with a free 'wee dram' at the end (motorists may take their drams away in a miniature bottle). Among the distilleries on the Trail are such famous malt whisky producers as Glenfiddich, whose malt whisky is one of the world's best-known, and Glenlivet, which was the first licensed distillery in the Highlands, established after the 1823 Act of Parliament aimed at cutting out illicit distilling and smuggling.

Another paradise for malt whisky lovers is the island of Islay, a two-hour ferry journey away from Kennacraig on the south-west coast of Kintyre. Islay's fame lies in its production of malt whiskies with uniquely wonderful smoky flavours. Some of Islay's best-known distilleries are congregated round Port Ellen, the port for the daily ferry from Kennacraig. Along the road which heads east out of Port Ellen to Claggain Bay you will find first the famous Laphroaig distillery, its white-washed buildings commanding a superb view of the coastline and sea, then the Lagavulin and Ardbeg distilleries. All three distilleries may be visited, though the Laphroaig distillery closes in July and August.

There was much illicit distilling and smuggling around Islay over the centuries, especially in The Oa, the windswept land jutting out into the sea west of Port Ellen. While little physical evidence of all this illegal activity remains, there is plenty to be seen of Islay's first legal distillery, set up at Bowmore in 1779 and still occupying its original buildings. Bowmore, Islay's administrative capital, lies north-west of Port Ellen on Loch Indaal. From the road between the two you may glimpse the Duich Moss peat bog, source of the peat which is essential to the flavour of Islay malt whiskies.

In the 19th century Campbeltown, on the west coast of Kintyre, boasted 34 malt whisky distilleries. Today there are only two producing the distinctive Campbeltown malts, and neither offers special guided tours for visitors. It is perhaps some consolation to know that even if the two did offer guided tours, you would not be able to buy malt whisky by the bottle there any cheaper than in other retail outlets: Scotland's distilleries must sell their product on site at the same retail prices as elsewhere.

OPPOSITE
The River Spey, near Garva Bridge in the Monadhliath mountains.

BELOW, LEFT
Inside the thoroughly modern Glenfiddich distillery, producer of one of Speyside's most popular malt whiskies. The distillery lies to the north of Dufftown, with its car park built beside the ruins of Balvenie Castle.

BELOW, RIGHT
The cask store at the Bruichladdich distillery, Islay. Whisky does not mature in bottles, so may remain for up to twenty years in casks like these before being bottled.

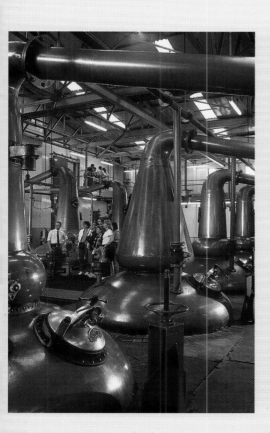

Chapter Four
The Highlands: the North-West

The north-west Highlands of Scotland include mainland Britain's most westerly point at Point of Ardnamurchan in the south-west and its most northerly point at Dunnet Head between Thurso and John o' Groats in the north-east. They also include its wildest, most scenically spectacular and most sparsely populated country in the great spread of land, much of it in Sutherland, which reaches towards Cape Wrath, the north-west tip of mainland Britain where long lochs like Erriboll and the Kyle of Durness in the north and lochs Inchard and Laxford round on the west coast cut deep into the land.

This extraordinary country is cut off from the rest of Britain by Glen Mor (or Glen Albyn), the Great Glen, a mighty landslip, formed some 350 million years ago, which is Britain's most impressive geological feature. The Great Glen contains a string of four lovely lochs, Ness, Oich, Lochy and Linnhe. The completion of the 60-mile-long Caledonian Canal in the 19th century, running from the sea at Loch Linnhe in the south-west to the sea of the Moray Firth in the north-west via all four lochs, effectively made north-west Scotland an island, for it provided a line of water the length of the Great Glen. The man-made part of the canal, for which James Watt was the surveyor and Thomas Telford the builder,

accounts for just 25 miles of its total length and is not as heavily used today as its pioneering builders imagined it would be.

Although the Caledonian Canal's draught is too shallow and its 29 locks too small to allow larger, working craft to use it to cut the distance from Scotland's west coast to the east, it is still much used by fishing boats and by pleasure craft whose owners want to enjoy the many pleasures of the Great Glen. These include, besides the lochs and canal, the ruins of various historically interesting castles, including Castle Urquhart on Loch Ness, near where the Loch Ness Monster is supposed to have his/her lair (as described at the Loch Ness Monster Centre at Drumnadrochit, a couple of miles up the road from the Castle), and Invergarry Castle, razed by 'Butcher' Cumberland after Culloden because its Jacobite owners had given shelter to Bonnie Prince Charlie.

Today, Invergarry's ruins provide the object of a pleasant before-dinner stroll in the grounds of the Glengarry Castle Hotel, one of those Victorian baronial piles, complete with glass cases of stuffed birds and tartan carpets, that help make touring in Scotland such a pleasant experience. The demands of holidaymakers since the mid-19th century have, of course, brought many changes here. The pleasant towns of Fort William, a major touring centre at the southern end of the Great Glen, and Fort Augustus, a popular angling centre at the

southern end of Loch Ness, both began life as forts built to pacify the Highland clans in their wild glens to the north. Even the good roads which take the touring motorist so quickly from place to place along the Great Glen follow, in places, the line of General Wade's Military Road which, reaching the Great Glen between the Grampian and Monadhliath mountains via the Corrieyairack Pass, crossed it near Fort Augustus.

Rising out of beautiful Glen Nevis south of Fort William, 1359m (4418ft) Ben Nevis, Britain's highest mountain, lures thousands of walkers, backpackers and climbers to its slopes every year, at the same time giving a foretaste of the spectacular scenery to come away to the north of the Great Glen.

Although it has hundreds of miles of good roads and plentiful links by sea and air, Scotland beyond the Great Glen still seems a world apart, a land of soaring mountain peaks, of rivers flowing over stony beds, of mighty waterfalls such as the 114m (370ft) Falls of Glomach in the Kintail Forest, of still, remote inland lochs, many of them with ruined castles on their shores attesting to a time when Highland clans and families were often at war with each other, and, on the west coast and in the far north, great sea lochs cutting into the land. Despite those ruined castles, the impression this country gives is one of nature and geography still paramount, of a land where people have made little impact.

It is a false impression, for parts of this country have been inhabited for longer than elsewhere in Britain, particularly on the fertile flatlands of the eastern, North Sea coasts. This is a country rich in prehistoric remains, from the Pictish brochs at Glenelg on the west coast, to the many cairns, burial chambers, brochs and field systems which dot the eastern coastal country, especially between Loch Brora and the coast at Brora, and in the country inland from Latheron and Lybster. At Achavanich, inland from Latheron on the A895, the 40 remaining Achavanich Standing Stones are of particular interest because of their oval, rather than circular, layout. A minor road off the A9 just beyond Lybster leads to the massive Grey Cairns of Camster, a complex layout of burial cairns dating back to the Stone and Bronze Ages which have been carefully restored.

On the eastern coast of the region, stretching north from Inverness, the 'Capital of the Highlands' at the top of the Great Glen on the Moray Firth, and the Black Isle right up to Duncansby Head, the land is a low-lying fertile strip backed, first by the hill country of Easter Ross, then by the brown moorland and flow, or marsh, country of the Caithness plateau. It is the country further west, broken by those great west coast sea lochs reaching far inland and marked by jagged mountain peaks rising from a strikingly underpopulated country that has led this part of mainland Britain to be called the last great wilderness in Europe.

Although Inverness, the headquarters of Highland Region, the largest local government region in Scotland, is the only major town of the region, there are numerous fine smaller towns, including Gairloch and Ullapool in the north-west, Thurso in the north and, over on the east coast, Dingwall, birthplace of Macbeth, on the Cromarty Firth, whose north shore has seen much new building connected with the North sea oil industry, Dornoch, home of the world's third oldest golf links, and Wick, which has been a royal burgh, albeit a small one, since the 12th century.

Strathpeffer, inland from Dingwall, became very popular in the 19th century as spa, pumping its water from sulphur and chalybeate springs. Today, it is a pleasant tourist centre, ideal for exploring Wester Ross where the highest peak is at Monro: 1056m (3433ft) Ben Wyvis.

Few other places in the north-west Highlands are big enough to counteract the impression that one is in a land where geography and nature, with its animal and bird life, is dominant over man. Lairg, at the east end of Loch Shin, is a pleasant market village at a crossroads of the Highlands whose August sheep sales are a major market for Sutherland's sheep farmers. But most people go there for the breathtakingly wild and beautiful country around it, most of them failing to notice that Loch Shin is, in fact, a reservoir and part of the Shin Valley hydro-electric scheme, one of the largest in the country. Tongue on the north coast? Again, an attractive little town with a good hotel and an essential garage and petrol station but it is the dramatic coastline with its wonderfully empty golden-sanded beaches and geological wonders like the Smoo Caves away to the west near Durness that bring people here, usually by way of Strathnaver or the road which skirts Loch Loyal

LEFT, BELOW
The farmland of Caithness stretches towards the Pentland Firth and the great sandstone promontory of Dunnet Head, the most northerly part of mainland Britain.

LEFT, ABOVE
Pleasure boats enjoy the peace of the Caledonian Canal at Fort Augustus. Named after Augustus, Duke of Cumberland, Fort Augustus was built after the 1715 Jacobite uprising. Today, it is a holiday town and popular angling centre.

RIGHT
A forestry plantation makes its mark on the hillside above Loch Lochy in Glen More, at the southern end of the Great Glen.

on its way up from Altnaharra, a village given importance by its well-known hotel.

It should not be forgotten, though, that while people and civilization do not look to have made a huge impact, outwardly at least, on this country, it has been inevitable that the 20th century should have brought many changes, the Shin Valley hydro-electric scheme and the vast acerages of the Forestry Commission's pine plantations among them.

The afforestation of the Flow Country of the north-west Highlands, much of it used as tax avoidance exercises by rich people, has caused much bitterness, conservationists and ecologists deploring the destructive march of the pine trees over peatland which has for centuries provided ideal habitats for many species of bird. The counter argument is that forestry helps the economy and provides jobs — and the Highlands need people. Two hundred years ago, about 20 per cent of the population of Scotland lived in the Highlands; today, the figure is about 5 per cent.

The reason why Strathnaver is so empty of people that you can drive all the way up its narrow unfenced road without needing to pull into a passing place to make space for another vehicle, is that this lovely valley was hit particularly hard during the Highland clearances, that infamous time in the early 19th century when landowners,

led by the 1st Duke of Sutherland based in his splendid Dunrobin Castle at Golspie on the east coast, cleared people out of their crofts and off the land to make way for sheep, deer and forestry. Bettyhill, on the coast north of Strathnaver and east of Tongue, was specially built by Elizabeth, Marchioness of Stafford, to house crofters evicted during the clearances. Another parish to suffer particularly badly during these evictions was Kildonan, near Helmsdale on the east coast, where almost four-fifths of the population disappeared from the Strath of Kildonan between 1801 and 1830.

On the plus side of the man/environment equation is the work being done by organizations like the much-maligned Forestry Commission, the Nature Conservancy and the National Trust for Scotland, to preserve this superb wilderness and to make its remote geography and wild nature accessible to people. At the impressive Corrieshalloch Gorge, south of Ullapool, for instance, where the Falls of Measach plunge 37 metres (120 feet) into the ravine, the National Trust for Scotland preserves a good observation platform and a suspension bridge built by John Fowler, the engineer of the Forth railway bridge.

While there are sanctuaries and reserves in many places – near Bettyhill, for instance, there is a bird sanctuary at Torrisdale Bay and the Invernaver Nature Reserve, with a fine collection of rare alpine plants, while the whole of tiny Handa Island, just offshore south of Loch Laxford, is one of Britain's most important bird sanctuaries. Nature is to be found at its most spectacular in north-west Scotland in areas like the Inverpolly Nature Reserve, at the Beinn Eighe National Nature Reserve, in Torridon, and at Inverewe Garden.

The Inverpolly Nature Reserve is in the far north-west, 10 miles by road north of Ullapool. Comprising 27,000 acres of virtually unpopulated mountain and loch wilderness with few trees or large plants, the Inverpolly reserve's habitats include marine islands, peat bog and moorland and birchwoods, providing shelter for wildcats, pinemartens, golden eagles and deer. Above them rise the jagged shapes of geologically ancient mountains, including Cul Beag, sugarloaf-shaped Suilven, and Stac Polly (or Pollaidh), whose splintered outline looks like some fairytale castle rising out of the land. There is fine fishing in many of the lochs of the reserve, especially Loch Sionascaig.

At the reserve's western edge, Knockan Cliff stretches for a mile above the road from Ullapool. Knockan Cliff is a geological rarity, a rock formation where the topmost layers of schists are older than the limestone and quartzite beneath, suggesting that tremendous upheavals of the land must have occurred here many millennia in the past. Knockan Cliff was turned into a nature trail

by the Nature Conservancy Council, who have marked out viewing points along a one-and-a-half-mile walk along it, many of them giving fine views over the Inverpolly Nature Reserve.

Quite different from the Inverpolly Reserve, because they are entirely the work of man, are the National Trust for Scotland's spectacular Inverewe Gardens, which lie at the head of the lovely sea loch, Loch Ewe, south-west of Loch Broom, the sea loch where Ullapool was founded as a fishing port in the late 18th century. Inverewe Gardens, a mile north of the village of Poolewe, were created just over a hundred years ago out of barren rock and today house a collection of some 2,500 plants, from alpine to subtropical, in a latitude further north than Moscow, a 'miracle' made possible by the Gulf Stream.

Loch Maree also lies south of Ullapool, inland

OPPOSITE, TOP
The ruins of Castle Urquhart brood over Loch Ness from the loch's western shore.

OPPOSITE, BOTTOM
Mainland Britain's northern coast reaches its most north-easterly point at Duncansby Head and the spectacular Stacks of Duncansby.

ABOVE, TOP
Ben Nevis, Britain's highest mountain, dominates the skyline beyond Fort William.

ABOVE
Ullapool, established as a fishing port in 1788, is now an attractive tourist centre and a main car ferry port for Stornoway on the Isle of Lewis.

OVERLEAF
Eilean Donan Castle, once a Jacobite stronghold.

from Gairloch, a popular holiday resort with a fine sandy beach superbly set on Loch Gairloch looking over the sea to the Outer Hebrides. Along Loch Maree's southern shore stretches the Beinn Eighe Nature Reserve, covering some 10,000 acres and named after one of the highest peaks here, 981m (3188ft) Beinn Eighe, one of five peaks in this area which rise above 923 metres (3000 feet). The Beinn Eighe Nature Reserve, the earliest of Britain's nature reserves, was set up in 1951 to preserve the remnants of the Caledonian Forest here.

The hand of man had fallen heavily on this ancient forest, with the Vikings felling trees for their ships and then burning any stands they did not want, and later warlords, including Robert the Bruce and Alexander Stewart, the Wolf of Badenoch, burning the forests to smoke out enemies or fugitives from justice. Today, not only is the forest in the Beinn Eighe reserve carefully preserved and made available for people to discover, via mountain trails and walks, but the land is also being replanted with Scots pine and native oak and birch.

From the high points of the Beinn Eighe mountain trail it is possible to get fine views along the 12-mile length of Loch Maree, the islands in the loch, including Isle Maree where the Irish St Maelrubha established a hermitage, and the wild mountain scenery away to the north, dominated by the 990m (3217ft) peak of Slioch, 'the spearhead'.

A drive south from Kinlochewe, a hill-walking, climbing and fishing base at the head of Loch Maree, to the village of Torridon on Upper Loch Torridon, brings one down Glen Torridon, one of Wester Ross's and, indeed, the whole Highlands', wildest glens – and, according to the National Trust for Scotland in whose care it is, one of its most beautiful, too. Both sides of the glen are lined with mountains which, being formed of horizontal strata of red Torridon sandstones, have a distinctive appearance, made all the more impressive by the stands of pine, remnants of the Caledonian Forest, which clothe headlands and lower mountain slopes.

Geologists have found that several of the peaks here are capped with white quartzite containing fossils of some of the first living creatures on Earth: an indication of how long these mountains have been in existence, being worn into their fantastic shapes by time and the erosion of wind and rain.

The National Trust for Scotland has established a countryside centre in Torridon which includes a deer museum and a fine audiovisual presentation of the wildlife to be found in Glen Torridon and the surrounding mountain country.

South of Torridon, the country takes on a new flavour. The beautiful, river-drained, mountain-surrounded glens are still here, including Glen Affric which, with the Dog Fall near the Affric

bridge, was one of the painter Landseer's favourite subjects, and Glenshiel, steeply enclosed by high mountains before the main road takes you past Shiel Bridge and between Loch Duich and the Five Sisters of Kintail.

History is beginning to intrude now, for military roads, old forts and ruined castles come up more frequently on the map. Among the most evocative of them is Eilean Donan Castle, built by Alexander II on an island at the meeting point of lochs Duich, Alsh and Long. Blown up by the English warship, *Worcester*, in 1719 because of the Jacobite sympathies of its owners, the MacRaes, the castle was rebuilt earlier this century by a later generation of MacRaes. The castle is a clear hint that for those wishing to follow in the footsteps of that most romantic figure in Scottish history, the Young Pretender, Prince Charles Edward Stuart, this is the part of the Highlands to come to first.

Bonnie Prince Charlie, coming from France in the brig *Du Taillay*, first set foot on Scottish soil on the tiny island of Eriskay on 23 July 1745. He reached the mainland, accompanied by just

seven men, on the shore of Loch nan Uamh two days later. By 19 August, those of the Highland clan leaders who chose to throw in their lot with the Stuart Prince had come with their men to Glenfinnan at the head of Loch Shiel to hear Charles proclaimed Regent for his father, James III and to see his standard raised.

The Glenfinnan Monument, a round tower topped with a statue of a kilted highlander, was erected at the spot in 1815 by Macdonald of Glenaladale, whose ancestor's support had been crucial to the Prince. The National Trust for Scotland maintains one of its interesting and informative Visitor Centres nearby.

ABOVE, TOP
The Glenfinnan Monument, Loch Shiel.

ABOVE
The Old Pretender presides at the baptism of his elder son, Prince Charles Edward Stuart.

OPPOSITE
The steep, jagged mass of Slioch towers over lovely Loch Maree.

OVERLEAF
Spectacular mountains and coasts: the Five Sisters of Kintail (page 56) and Sango Bay near Durness in Sutherland (page 57).

From Glenfinnan, Bonnie Prince Charlie's great adventure took him up the Great Glen, via Fort William (built by William III to help prevent such Jacobite risings as the Prince was now engaged upon) and Invergarry and so into the south, where he stayed at Blair Castle, in Perth, where he proclaimed his father king, and in Stirling, where his army took the town but not the castle. By 17 September, the Prince was in Edinburgh, where, having again taken the city but not the castle, he stayed until early November. While he was in Edinburgh, the Jacobite army achieved a confidence-boosting victory over a Government force at Preston Pans on 21 September.

By mid-November Bonnie Prince Charlie and his army were in England, where Carlisle fell to him after a five-day siege. On 4 December, the Prince reached Derby, stayed two days surveying his situation with his generals — and then began the retreat to Scotland which ended in crushing defeat at Culloden on 16 April 1746. The Scots, starving and exhausted, lost 1200 of their 5000 men while only 76 of King George II's 10,000 redcoats, led by his son the Duke of Cumberland, were killed.

For nearly five months after Culloden the

fugitive Prince Charles Edward Stuart and his dwindling band of supporters hid out in the homes of loyal clansmen, in caves and out in the open in the Highlands, on Skye and the islands of the Outer Hebrides as they waiting for a ship from France to rescue them. Although there was a price of £30,000, a huge sum in those days, on his head, and although the victor of Culloden, the Duke of Cumberland pursued him relentlessly, no-one betrayed the Prince. On 19 September 1746 he left Scotland from the same loch shore he had arrived on in July 1745, never to return.

After Culloden, the way of life of the peoples of the Highlands changed forever. Hitherto, they had lived in small communities in a near-feudal society existing mainly on cattle-breeding and in which loyalty to a laird or chief who could provide a force to protect the cattle was paramount. Now the Hanoverian government set out to destroy this militant society. Firearms and the kilt (a martial dress and a badge of loyalty) were proscribed and the old legal powers of the clan chiefs were abolished. Gradually, life became more prosperous and more settled in the Highlands. Money rents began to replace feudal dues, new crops were introduced and capitalists from both Scotland and England began sinking

money into projects such as fishing harbours and ports (for example, Ullapool, established by the British Fisheries Society in 1788), iron foundries and woollen mills. At the same time, the far-sighted Prime Minister, William Pitt, began a system of recruiting the young men of the clans into the British Army, where the Highland regiments were soon an outstanding force.

Ironically, it was the defeat of Napoleon at Waterloo, in which the Highland regiments played a glorious role, and the end of the Napoleonic Wars that brought severe depression to the Highlands, a major result of which was the Clearances to make way for large farms for sheep, the only form of farming that would bring in any profit. Many of the Highland's crofters moved south to the industrial cities of the Lowlands; many more emigrated to the United States or to the British colonies in Canada, Australia and New Zealand. The population figures in the Highlands have never returned to what they were before the Clearances, and the land is still very much worked in large estates where forestry, fish farming, deer hunting and grouse shooting, along with tourism, play major roles in the economy.

Clans and Tartans

No visitor to Scotland can remain unaware for long of how important to the Scottish tourist industry is the whole business of clan history and tartans. Outside gift and souvenir shops along the Royal Mile in Edinburgh, flapping in the breeze, are brightly coloured maps of Scotland, dozens of surnames printed across them: here your ancestors lived, here is the tartan you may like to wear. Inside the shop are piles of tins of shortbread biscuits or cream fudge, decorated with gaudy tartans surrounding a picture of Bonnie Prince Charlie or Robbie Burns. Down the street other shops are full of Scottish knitwear, racks of tartan kilts, trews, scarves, hose and all the extras needed to kit yourself out as a full-blooded Highlander.

It is fashionable to deplore all this 'tartanry', dismissing it as an unattractive outcome of the modern tourist business, demeaning to the real character of Scotland.

Behind it all, however, lies some historical reality. The word 'clann' is Gaelic for 'family' or 'children', and refers to a system which can be traced back in Scottish life for many centuries. The idea of a clan began to have meaning round about the 6th century, when the Scots were spreading through the whole of the country, displacing earlier tribes. When powerful individuals took over parcels of land, they also acquired the people living there; later on, some of these powerful men carving themselves small empires out of Scottish land were not even Scots: the Bruces and the Cummings were both descended from Norman knights who had come to England with William the Conqueror.

In time, the clan system developed characteristics which set it apart from other social forms. Because the life of the Highland Scots depended on cattle, defending the cattle from outsiders was essential; the men of a clan, not needed for farming, became clansmen,

giving their chief an absolute (and willing) loyalty. A clan chief counted his wealth not in terms of rent but in terms of clansmen he could call out. He could also establish the laws which governed life on his land. Loyalty to the clan was paramount over loyalty to the king and while the clans often fought each other, in time, as the kings of Scotland began parcelling out land to 'buy' loyalty, clans who had held the land for generations found it necessary to fight those who had been granted it by the king.

The costume which these clans wore began as simple garments, held round the waist with a belt and with a long end thrown over the shoulders, which acted as covering, blanket and shelter from the weather. The plaid, a warm woollen cloth dyed with vegetable dyes, did not reach Scotland until wool became available. At first the fabric was dyed in colours which indicated the rank of the wearer, then the district he came from, and, finally, the clan to which he belonged. Although the Scottish scholar and poet, George Buchanan, noted in the 16th century that the Highlander delighted in wearing 'variegated garments, especially stripes in their favourite colours of purple and blue', it was not until around 1700 that the distinctive tartan patterns, or setts, began to be developed. Different districts in the Highlands developed different setts, which really only became associated with a particular clan because that clan dominated the district in which the tartan was woven.

It was early in the 18th century, too, that the one-piece plaid came to be made in two halves, the bottom section gathered round the waist becoming the permanently pleated kilt, and the top section becoming a separate garment.

During the 36 years that the wearing of tartan was proscribed after the Battle of Culloden, most of the old setts, carefully marked on sticks by the women who wove them, were lost, so that the majority of the tartans we know today are of 19th-century origin. The man most responsible for bringing them back into favour was the hugely successful writer, Sir Walter Scott. His romantic novels, read all over Europe, made Scottish history immensely popular, while the admiration felt for the tartan-clad Highland regiments of the British Army made the fabric a fashionable item.

Sir Walter Scott was, in effect, the first great public relations figure in Scottish history. He instigated the hunt for the Regalia of Scotland (it was found in a cupboard in Edinburgh Castle, where it had lain forgotten since 1707) and he organized the successful State Visit of George IV to Scotland in 1822, during which the king, staying at the Palace of Holyroodhouse, attended functions wearing Royal Stewart tartan.

After George IV's visit, the demand for tartan reached such heights that the weavers supplying Edinburgh's tartan salesmen had to install dozens more looms. The fashion was given a boost when Queen Victoria and Prince Albert, furnishing their new castle at Balmoral, had a special Balmoral tartan designed which was used for much of the carpets and furnishings and which the royal children wore. Today, when they are in Scotland, the members of the Royal Family still wear their own tartan, in kilts for the men, pleated skirts for the women.

For all those without a tartan, there is no need to despair, for there are plenty to choose from, and no rules forbidding their wearing. The Museum of Scottish Tartans at Comrie, near Crieff in Perthshire, holds more than 1300 tartan setts belonging to the Scottish Tartans Society as well as a fine collection of everything to do with the making and wearing of tartan. The collection of tartans made by the historian of Scottish dress, J. Telfer Dunbar, is housed in the Canongate Tolbooth in Edinburgh.

Aspects of the modern tartan industry. Tartan may be worn by men and women, with military uniforms or with everyday dress.

OPPOSITE
The uniform plaid is held in place by a large brooch mounted with a cairngorm, a yellow or brown ornamental quartz traditionally used in Scottish jewellery.

ABOVE, TOP
A properly made man's kilt is a very expensive item, requiring many yards of material and hours of labour, including a great deal of handwork.

ABOVE
Clans may have several tartan setts, or patterns, with their names, such as 'dress' tartans, usually light in colour and worn by the women of the clan, 'hunting' tartans which are darker and intended to camouflage the wearer, and 'ancient' tartans; there may also be different tartan setts for different branches of a clan. The two tartans illustrated here are Ancient Campbell (left) and MacDonald.

Chapter Five
South-West Scotland

The gently green and rolling hill country which makes up much of Scotland's south-west is bounded in the north by hill country of a more 'Highland' character cut across by Glen Dochart, Glen Lochy and the Pass of Brander, which the A85 follows on its way west to the eastern shore of Loch Linnhe and the Firth of Lorn, where is the coastal town and ferry terminal of Oban. In the south the boundary is the coast running east from the Mull of Galloway along the Solway Firth. In the west, the northern part of the coast is as broken and indented and sprinkled with offshore islands as it is all the way to Cape Wrath, with the Kintyre peninsula and Knapdale forming a sheltering arm for the islands of Arran and Bute in the Firth of Clyde. South of the Clyde the coast, unbroken by sea lochs and dotted with popular seaside resorts and famous

golf courses such as Ardrossan, Troon, Turnberry, Ayr and Girvan, curves down to the hammerhead peninsula of The Rhinns of Galloway.

Within this area, covered by two local government regions, Strathclyde and Dumfries and Galloway, are Scotland's most industrialized and heavily populated area, Clydeside, including Britain's third largest city, Glasgow; its most popular holiday areas, the Trossachs and the islands of the Firth of Clyde; and the country, Ayrshire, where both Scotland's hero Robert the Bruce and its favourite son and finest poet, Robbie Burns, were born and where Burns wrote most of his finest poetry. Another less heroic figure in Scottish history, the cattle rustler Rob Roy MacGregor, who was turned into a romantic Robin Hood figure in Sir Walter Scott's eponymous novel, also came from south-west

Scotland; his home, and the places were the MacGregors hid their stolen cattle, was in the north of the area, beyond the head of Loch Fyne, and he is buried at Balquidder, north of Loch Katrine.

While this is the most heavily populated part of Scotland, with half of all the country's people living in Glasgow and its satellite towns, from Johnstone and Paisley in the west to Airdrie and Motherwell in the east, it also has its share of lovely countryside, marked with glens and lochs, including Loch Lomond, Loch Katrine and Loch Trool; country and forest parks, including the Argyll, Queen Elizabeth and Galloway Forest Parks and the Culzean Country Park; and bird sanctuaries and nature reserves. The great rock of Ailsa Craig, 10 miles out to sea off Girvan, is an important breeding place for birds, and Troon's

offshore island, Lady Isle, is a bird sanctuary. The Forestry Commission maintains two of its three tree gardens in Scotland in Argyll.

It is a region with a good share of the country's most famous castles, too. There are the Campbells' ruined Kilchurn Castle at the head of Loch Awe and their magnificent, 18th-century Inveraray on Loch Fyne. Set high above the Clyde just before it reaches Glasgow is Bothwell Castle, a 13th-century stronghold, whose red sandstone curtain walls are set with round towers; further up the Clyde, west of Lanark, is Craignethan Castle, an impressive moated fortress built in the 16th century. Down on the Ayrshire coast are the Kennedy of Cassilis family's legend-surrounded ruins of Dunure Castle and, in complete contrast, the same family's magnificent Culzean Castle, a supreme example of the work of Robert Adam. In Dumfries and Galloway are moated Caelaverock Castle on the Solway Firth, its fine Renaissance interior facade the work of its 17th-century owner, Lord Nithsdale, head of the Maxwell clan, and, away to the north of Dumfries in Nithsdale, the magnificent Jacobean pile of Drumlanrig Castle, with a superb Rembrandt among its many treasures. Grim Threave Castle, a 14th-century stronghold of the Douglas family, is in Galloway, near Castle Douglas.

As the River Tweed dominates the Borders, the eastern side of the Scottish Lowlands, so the Clyde, rising within a mile of the Tweed in the Southern Uplands dominates the western side of the Lowlands. A third river, the Annan, also rises in the same hills, though it flows south to reach the sea at the Solway Firth.

In its upper reaches, the Clyde can be as lovely a river as the Tweed. There is the gentle little stream, rising in the hills 80 miles south-east of Glasgow. There is the quietly pretty scenery of Clydesdale, an area of many market gardens and orchards which gave its name to the Clydesdale horse, many of which are still bred, along with Aberdeen Angus cattle, in the farms around Biggar, a delightful town, medieval in origin, on the border of Clydesdale and Tweeddale. And there is the Clyde Gorge, with waterfalls like the 27.7m (90ft) fall of Cora Linn, one of the Falls of Clyde in the gorge, which is near New Lanark, the industrial model village founded in 1784 by David Dale, a philanthropic cotton mill owner. Once in North Lanarkshire, the Clyde is a major waterway, providing the water which once powered the industrial heart of Scotland and which still plays a major role in the new Glasgow.

It was in the early 1780s that Glasgow began its extraordinarily rapid transformation into one of the great industrial cities of the world. Already prosperous through New World trade, including the tobacco trade with Virginia and Maryland, Glasgow grabbed the opportunities of the Industrial Revolution with both hands, turning to cotton production based on immigrant labour, first from the Highlands and then from Ireland (in the process creating what would become in the 19th century some of the worst slums and areas of social deprivation in Britain). In the 1780s, the Clyde was deepened and widened where it flowed through central Glasgow to take larger river traffic to deal with the new trade. Then came the age of the steam

engine, bringing the ship builders, who based themselves downriver at Clydebank, the heavy engineering works and the steel makers, their factories and workshops powered by coal from the Lanark coalfields.

In Glasgow today there is little to be found of the medieval seat of learning that was the old Glasgow, apart from the fine 12th- and 13th-century Cathedral, built on the site of St Mungo's 6th-century church, and Provand's Lordship, the oldest domestic building in Glasgow, built in 1470 to house the priest in charge of a nearby hospital.

Most of Glasgow today, with its amazing skyline of factories, towerblocks, chimneys and the occasional church spire, is either Victorian or very modern, for Glasgow's second miraculous makeover has occurred in our time. The city has overcome the devastation of its industrial base and the deaths of its great industries, rebuilding its worst slum areas and turning itself into what has been called 'Europe's first post-industrial city' as well as one of its big cultural centres.

Glasgow is a vibrant, lively place, the home of Scottish Opera and the Scottish National Orchestra, and a city where, among the big shops in Argyle, Sauchiehall and Buchanan Streets, you can find such gems as the Charles Rennie Mackintosh-designed Willow Tea Rooms in Sauchiehall Street and, in nearby Renfrew Street,

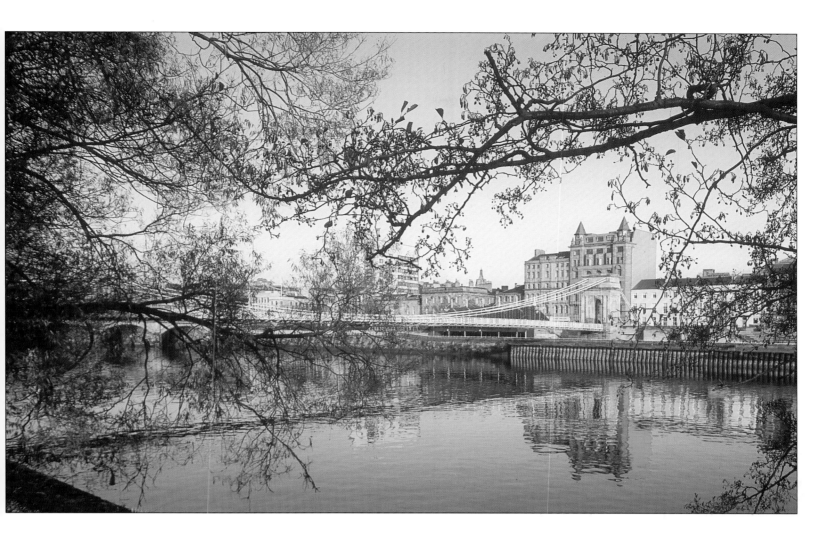

his masterpiece, the Glasgow School of Art. Go away from the centre, to Glasgow Green, one of the city's many fine parks, and you'll find the People's Palace, devoted to the social history of Glasgow. Further way, in Pollock Park, is the Burrell Museum, a wonderfully light and airy glass-walled building housing the art collection of the shipping magnate Sir William Burrell. Since the museum was opened in 1983 it has become Scotland's top tourist attraction, getting more visitors every year than any other tourist site in the country.

For Glaswegians wanting a holiday or just a day or so out of the city, two of Scotland's most popular holiday areas, the islands of the Firth of Clyde with the Kintyre peninsula to their west, and The Trossachs, are hardly any distance away, the one downriver where the Clyde widens out into the great Firth of Clyde, the other away to the north-west, where Loch Lomond reaches up into the hills of Argyll.

Kintyre, the Cowal peninsula and the Firth of Clyde islands, especially Arran and Bute, make a natural playground for all of western Strathclyde, easily reached from Glasgow and within good steamer services of the southern islands of the Inner Hebrides. The many lochs and streams, both on the mainland and the islands, attract fishermen hoping for salmon, trout and sea-trout, while the

calm, sheltered waters of the Kyles of Bute are ideal for holiday cruising and sailing.

Arran, largest of the Firth of Clyde islands, has been called 'Scotland in Miniature' because of the fine mixture of lochs, glens, streams and mountains, including 882m (2868ft) Goatfell, which make up its scenery, especially in the north. Its attractive coastline is cut by many bays, some sandy, some rocky, and many giving sheltered anchorage to sailing boats. Busiest of the bays is Brodick Bay, dominated by 15th-century Brodick Castle, owned by the National Trust for Scotland, and with spectacular gardens, including a fine collection of rhododendrons. Brodick, at the southern end of the bay, is Arran's main port, where the ferries from Ardrossan come in, and a holiday centre.

Near the west coast resort of Blackwaterfoot are cairns built in the Bronze Age and the King's Caves, so-called because they gave shelter to Robert the Bruce when he returned from exile in Ireland. They are just two of the many sites which help make Arran a walkers' paradise, as well as a mecca for birdwatchers and for geologists, who come because just about every rock type may be found on Arran.

Bute, at the foot of the Cowal peninsula and flatter and more fertile than Arran, is quieter, too, but just as popular with Glaswegians: not for

ABOVE
Among the dozen bridges which span the Clyde in central Glasgow is this elegant suspension bridge, dating from 1871.

OPPOSITE, TOP
Loch Katrine seen from the summit of Ben A'An, at the eastern end of the loch in the Trossachs.

OPPOSITE, BOTTOM
Street musicians enliven the day in Buchanan Street, at the heart of Glasgow's shopping area, during the city's annual May Fest.

PAGE 64
Inveraray Castle, at Inveraray on Loch Fyne, is the seat of the dukes of Argyll, heads of Clan Campbell.

PAGE 65, TOP
In Glen Trool, Dumfries and Galloway.

PAGE 65, BOTTOM
Fishing boats tied up in the harbour at Kirkcudbright, an ancient Stewartry burgh and now an artists' colony on the Dee Estuary.

PAGES 66-7
The gaunt ruins of 14th-century Threave Castle, on an islet in the River Dee, was once a stronghold of the Black Douglases, so called to distinguish them from a light-haired branch of the clan called the Red Douglases.

nothing has 'The Day We Went to Rothesay-O!' long been a popular music hall song, revived for the television age by the late Andy Stewart. Rothesay is Bute's main town, reached by ferry from Wemyss Bay. Still surrounded by its deep moat, Rothesay Castle, once owned by the Stuart kings, has been a ruin since Cromwell destroyed it in the 17th century.

From Arran there are summertime ferries to Kintyre and from Bute across the Kyles of Bute to the Cowal peninsula. Here, back on the mainland, one can very quickly head north to be in the remote, little populated mountain and forest country which characterizes much of Argyll. Stretching up the shores of Loch Long and across much of the north-east section of the Cowal peninsula almost as far west as Loch Fyne is the great Argyll Forest Park, the first to be established by the Forestry Commission in Britain.

Loch Fyne is Campbell country. Near the head of the loch, on the west shore, is the elegant town of Inveraray, where Inveraray Castle, on the banks of the River Aray, has been the main fortress and home of the Campbell clan since the 15th century. The present castle dates from the 18th century and was built for the 3rd Duke of Argyll by William Adam and Robert Morris. For those interested in discovering the land of Rob

Roy, there is a walk of about 5 miles from the castle grounds up Glen Shira to the Falls of Aray and the home, now a ruin, of Rob Roy.

The heart of Rob Roy MacGregor country is not here, however, but in The Trossachs, Glasgow's other favourite playground. The Trossachs, which first became a fashionably romantic place to visit in the 18th century is, strictly speaking, just the short gorge linking two lovely lochs, Achray and Katrine. But the name has come to be given to the much wider region of lochs, rugged hills and streams tumbling over stony beds which stretches west from the attractive resort of Callander, at the foot of the Pass of Leny just 15 miles from Stirling, as far as Loch Lomond. The latter is Scotland's largest inland loch, stretching 23 miles from the outer suburbs of Glasgow almost to the edge of the Highlands.

Aberfoyle, lying between the Lake of Menteith (Scotland's only 'lake') and Loch Ard, is generally considered the main gateway to The Trossachs and to the Rob Roy country which embraces lochs Ard, Chon, Venacher, Achray and Katrine. It is an attractive little town out of season, but at the height of summer can be overwhelmed by the numbers of tourists and coaches which descend on it. But Aberfoyle is also at the centre of the Queen Elizabeth Forest

Park, which is more than big enough to absorb thousands of visitors into its miles of forest paths, mountain walks, including ones up 729m (2369ft) Ben Venue and 876m (2847ft) Ben Ledi, and its picnic areas without losing the attraction of its remote mountain and loch atmosphere.

Both the main lochs of The Trossachs, Katrine and Lomond, offer boat trips in the summer, those on Loch Katrine being on the famous Dumbarton-built steamer, *Sir Walter Scott* — aptly named because it was Sir Walter Scott who first drew the world's attention to the loveliness of the loch in *The Lady of the Lake*: the lady was the beautiful Ellen Douglas, after whom Ellen's Isle at the eastern end of the loch is named.

Sir Walter Scott never penetrated very far into Ayrshire or Dumfriesshire, south of Glasgow, partly because the Border country to the east was where he was happiest, but partly, perhaps, because he was very much aware of the overwhelming influence of the spirit of Robert Burns in this land.

Robert Burns, the son of a poor farmer, was born in Alloway, then a small village near Ayr, in 1759 and died in Dumfries in 1796. Apart from short stays in Edinburgh, where the youthful Walter Scott, meeting him at a party, was greatly impressed by the strength of his personality, and tours of the Borders and the Highlands, Burns spent all his life in Ayrshire and in Dumfries, where his work as an excise officer took him into all parts of the shires in what is now the local government region of Dumfries and Galloway.

Because most of his poetry grew out of his own emotions and his intense feelings for the lives of people close to him and for his country, Scotland, Robert Burns did not need the sight of spectacularly beautiful scenery to spur his genius — though he did write some very fine verse while on his epic 600-mile tour of the beautiful Highland country east of the Great Glen. The quiet farming country of Ayrshire, with its green, rolling hills and its gently flowing streams was inspiration enough for some of his finest lyric poetry, while for his more rumbustious songs, what better inspiration could there be than the snug, warm, friend-filled rooms of the inns and pubs he stayed in while riding over his excise-collecting routes in Dumfriesshire and Galloway?

Both shires, while rich in relics of Robert Burns' life and work, especially in Alloway, where much of the village is given over to the Robert Burns Heritage Park, and in Dumfries, where the house in which he spent the last years of his life is at the heart of the town's tourist trail, have much else to offer the visitor.

An attractive feature of the area is that in few parts is it ever crowded. While much of the inland countryside is quiet farming land, with pleasant but hardly compelling scenery, down in the south there are many places of outstanding natural history interest, like the sea-bird colony at Balcary Point on Balcary Bay, or the National Scenic Area at the Nith Estuary on the Solway

Firth, where the Nature Conservancy Council has a nature reserve at Kirkconnell Flow, which is a rare raised peat bog.

The Solway Firth, today a place of quiet towns and small villages, their harbours still sheltering fishing boats, is rich in the reminders of historic events. Among quietly attractive towns to visit along or just inland from the coast, are Annan on the Solway Firth, ancient Dumfries, built on the banks of the Nith, and Kirkcudbright, since the late 19th century a lively artists' colony in the ancient Stewartry land, so-called because in the 15th century, the kings of Scotland wrested the rule of the area from its ancient chiefs and put it in the hands of royal stewards. Near Kirkcudbright is one of those historic reminders: the ruins of Dundrennan Abbey. In this Cistercian Abbey, on

15/16 May 1568, Mary, Queen of Scots spent her last night in Scotland. Having escaped from Loch Leven, only for her supporters to be defeated at Langside, near Glasgow, she came here hoping to get help from her cousin, Elizabeth of England. No word coming from England, the Queen of Scots decided to go to England anyway, and boarded a boat at Port Mary, landing on the Cumberland coast. All that was ahead of her was nearly twenty years of imprisonment, ended by her execution.

The far west of Dumfries and Galloway, an almost forgotten corner of Scotland, has a coast of cliffs and sandy beaches washed by the warm Gulf Stream, the cliffs being particularly rugged at the Mull of Galloway. Wigtown on the Machars peninsula, Glenluce on the Water of Luce, where the wizard Michael Scot is supposed to have entrapped the Plague in a vault of Glenluce Abbey in the 13th century, and, in the far west on the Rhinns of Galloway, the popular holiday town of Portpatrick are just three of the many interesting places on a coast just made for quiet pottering.

Go inland, however, and things become more dramatic. Not only are there the lovely Eskdale, Annandale and Nithsdale, all three of them with interesting towns and villages, old castles and even prehistoric remains to explore, but in the Galloway Forest Park there is much satisfyingly remote and wild country as well. Around Loch Trool, in steeply wooded Glen Trool, where the Buchan Burn has to plunge over the rocks of the Buchan Falls before reaching Loch Trool, are miles of invigorating walks. It was in this area that Robert the Bruce had a famous victory over an English army in 1307; from Bruce's Stone, overlooking the loch and the battle site on the far shore, there are fine views of the Galloway Hills.

Robert Burns, the Ploughman Poet

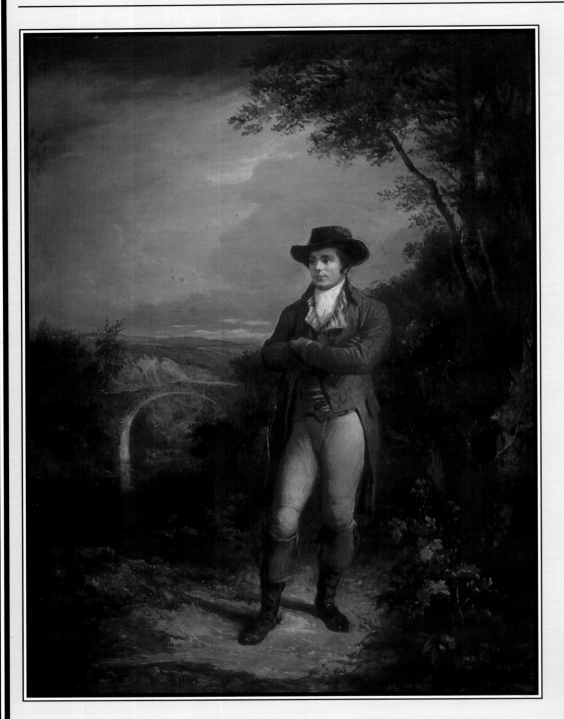

small thatched cottage that was to be his family's home for more than seven years. It still exists, carefully restored and lovingly cared for at the heart of the Burns National Heritage Park in Alloway, a recent bringing together of all the elements in the Burns connection in Alloway, completed in time for it to be at the centre of the celebrations of the Burns' bicentenary in 1996.

Within the Burns National Heritage Park are the Burns Cottage, with a museum containing a treasure house of relics and memorabilia next door; The Tam o' Shanter Experience, which includes the former Land o' Burns Centre and two audio-visual theatres using multi-media techniques to introduce visitors to Robert Burns and his life, and then to tell the story of Tam o' Shanter, one of Burns' liveliest creations; the Burns Monument, also a small museum, set in fine gardens; and the Auld Brig o' Doon, across which Tam was chased by the witches from the Auld Kirk, whose ruins are also in the Heritage Park.

In the centre of Ayr itself are other connections with Robert Burns, including the attractive old inn which Burns used as the setting for the convivial evening of merrymaking that was nearly Tam o' Shanter's downfall.

Other places within a radius of a few miles of Ayr which Burns knew well include Tarbolton,

Robert Burns is Scotland's national poet, one of the world's finest lyric poets and a man so in tune with the feelings and aspirations of his fellow men that, two hundred years after his death, he is revered all over the world, with his birthday, 25 January, being kept as a special day of celebration by Scots – and non-Scots – everywhere.

Although Burns' admirers may find relics and reminders of him in many parts of Scotland, particularly along the routes of his two great tours through Scotland, one of which took him round the Border country in search of Scottish songs and

poetry, and one of which took him on a 600-mile route through the Highlands of Scotland, it is to south-west Scotland, especially Ayrshire and Dumfriesshire, that people come from all over the world to discover for themselves what Robert Burns, often called the Ploughman Poet, was really like.

Among the many places in Ayrshire with which Burns had connections, none is more important that the small village of Alloway, now a suburb of Ayr, where he was born in 1759, the eldest son of a poor farmer, William Burnes, and his wife, Agnes. William Burnes himself built the

OPPOSITE, LEFT
This famous portrait of Robert Burns, painted by Alexander Nasmyth, was done from life while the poet was living in Edinburgh in 1786-7

OPPOSITE, RIGHT
The Burns Monument in Allloway, the village where he was born in 1759

ABOVE
Alloway's Brig O' Doon, where Robert Burns set the climax of his roistering tale, Tam O'Shanter. In Burns' day this was the main bridge over the Doon at Alloway, so that Tam naturally rode his horse over it at a gallop; today the bridge is reserved for walkers only.

the nearest village to Lochlea Farm, the Burns family's second financially unrewarding venture into farming, Kirkoswald, Mauchline, and Irvine. At Tarbolton, Robert Burns and his younger brother Gilbert joined together with like-minded friends to form the Bachelors' Club, an agreeable society where they could all come together to discuss important issues of the day, or just to have sociable get-togethers. The club was in a hall, also used for dancing classes which the Burns boys joined, next to an inn, which they also frequented. On a more serious note, Robert Burns took his first degrees in Freemasonary at Tarbolton. The Bachelors' Club, in the care of the National Trust for Scotland, is now an important stopping point on the Burns trail in Ayrshire.

So, too, is a thatched cottage in Kirkoswald, also in the care of the National Trust for Scotland. This is Souter Johnnie's Cottage, called after the souter (or cobbler) who was Tam o' Shanter's cronie. Burns based Souter Johnie on his friend John Davidson, a souter who lived in the Kirkoswald cottage.

The other main centre of interest for

followers of Robert Burns is in Dumfries, where the poet spent the last years of his life, from 1788 until his death in 1796, while working as an Excise officer. His work took him to many of the towns of Dumfries and Galloway, so that all over this attractive part of south-west Scotland are places where, often unexpectedly, one can come across reminders of the poet.

The most evocative of the Dumfries connections with Robert Burns are the house in the centre of the town in which he lived with his wife, Jean Armour and their children, and the Globe Inn, Burns' favourite howff, where visitors may see the chair Burns usually occupied.

These are more appropriate places to try to recall the real Robert Burns than, say, his mausoleum in the churchyard at Dumfries, for Robert Burns was a man who loved life and good fellowship, and who believed that

'For a' that, an' a' that,
It's coming yet for a' that,
That man to man the world o' er
Shall brother be for a' that.'

Chapter Six
Scotland's Islands

Scotland's many islands lie in the Atlantic Ocean strung along the west coast and above the northern coast, stretching far up into the sub-arctic waters where the Atlantic Ocean meets the Norwegian Sea. Scotland's east coast has virtually no islands at all.

Modern transport means that the islands, even remote St Kilda, are not as cut-off from mainland Scotland as once they were. Efficient car ferry and shipping services link the islands with the mainland and with each other, though some of the smaller and more remote ferry links operate only in the summer, and airfields and runways, large and small, are scattered throughout the islands. The North Sea oil industry has, of course, brought very sophisticated helicopter and aeroplane services to Shetland and Orkney as well as to the mainland.

Sometimes 'progress' is not always universally welcomed. The large Inner Hebridean island of Skye got a bridge to replace the centuries-old Kyle of Lochalsh-Kyleakin ferry in 1995. Many people protested, partly because the tolls charged for all wheeled traffic using the bridge were the highest in Europe, and partly because the bridge was seen as destroying the independence of an island which Dr Johnson, visiting it with James Boswell in the late 18th century, thought the finest of all the Scottish islands he had seen and which, more recently, the Gaelic poet, Sorley Maclean described as 'the great beautiful bird of Scotland'. For a time, stories of an Ealing Comedy situation (*Whisky Galore*, perhaps, in which the residents of a small island won out against the rules and regulations of officialdom) prevailing in Skye filtered out into the national press; lorry loads of sheep, readers of *The Times* were told, were being unloaded on one side of the bridge, driven across on foot and reloaded into another lorry on the other side, thus neatly avoiding the tolls.

The Skye residents' attitude to the new bridge is typical of the independence of the people who live on Scotland's islands — not that everyone there regards themselves as automatically of Scotland; it's not unusual to hear people in Lewis in the Outer Hebrides, for instance, refer to the mainland, not as the mainland, but as Scotland, another country.

Scotland's islands fall into five well-defined groups, with other islands scattered among them. Stretches of often stormy seas ranging from the large — the Pentland Firth, the North Minch and Little Minch — to the small, like the Sound of

Sleat where the winter gales were often strong enough to stop the Skye ferry and may well close the new bridge, separate them from each other and from the mainland.

Lying quite close to the mainland in a string some 150 miles long are the Inner Hebrides. The large island, Skye, which has the islands of Rona, Raasay and Scalpay lying off its east coast, is the northernmost of the Inner Hebrides and Islay, off the Kintyre peninsula and the source of some of Scotland's finest malt whiskies, is the most southerly. Between these two are one more large island, Mull with its attendant islands of Staffa and Iona, and numerous smaller islands, including the splendidly named Canna, Rhum, Eigg, Muck, Coll and Tiree. To the north of Islay are Jura and Colonsay.

To the south of the Inner Hebrides, another group of islands, including Arran, Bute and Cumbrae, lie in the comparative quiet of the Clyde estuary and have been included in this book in the chapter on south-west Scotland, which includes Glasgow and the Clyde.

Reaching further out into the stormy waters of the North Atlantic are the Outer Hebrides, or Western Isles. These wind-swept islands stretch for 130 miles from the Butt of Lewis at the top of the most northerly island, Lewis, to Barra Head at the southern tip of Barra. The islands in the group are Lewis and Harris, which together make up Britain's largest offshore island, in the north, North Uist, Benbecula and South Uist, which are

linked by a causeway, and Barra (the island on which *Whisky Galore* was filmed in 1948). The only big town in the Outer Hebrides is Stornoway, on the east coast of Lewis.

As in the Inner Hebrides, there are numerous smaller islands, islets and barren reefs off the bigger islands in the Western Isles. Among the most memory-charged of them is tiny Eriskay, a short ferry ride from the southern tip of South Uist. This was the place where Bonnie Prince Charlie first set foot in Scotland in 1745; it was also the island on which the whisky-laden SS *Politician* went aground a couple of hundred years later, inspiring Compton Mackenzie's novel *Whisky Galore*. The lovely Gaelic melody, 'The Eriskay Love Lilt', celebrates the romance of Bonnie Prince Charlie rather than Compton Mackenzie's comedy. (In that other well-known song about Bonnie Prince Charlie, 'The Skye Boat Song', the place from which the bonnie boat was speeding over the sea to Skye was Benbecula, not the Scottish mainland.)

Far out in the Atlantic, 45 miles west of North Uist, lies the St Kilda group of four islands and numerous islets. The islands' population became so reduced early this century that in 1930 the remaining inhabitants on Hirta, the largest island, asked to be evacuated. Today the islands, in the care of the National Trust for Scotland and the Nature Conservancy Council, are largely sanctuaries for birds, including the world's largest colony of gannets.

Orkney and Shetland lie above Scotland's north coast. The Orkney group is the nearest to the mainland, some six to eight miles north of the coast at John O' Groats and separated from it by the Pentland Firth, in which the Island of Stroma offers sanctuary to colonies of seals. There are about 70 islands and islets in the Orkney group, only about a third of them inhabited. Foremost among them is Mainland, with the Orkney capital and main harbour, Kirkwall, at its heart. Other Orkney islands, scattered between South Ronaldsay in the south and North Ronaldsay in the north, include Hoy, Flotta, Shapinsay, Stronsay, Rousay, Eday, Westray and Sanday. On the whole, the islands of Orkney are low-lying, largely treeless and not particularly 'scenic', though they more than make up for this by the wealth of pre-historic remains and monuments scattered across them.

Sixty miles of often rough sea separate Orkney from Shetland, with Fair Isle, one of   the Shetland islands and famed for its bird sanctuaries and knitting patterns, lying between the two groups.

Shetland has an even higher ratio of uninhabited to inhabited islands than Orkney, with only twelve of its near-one hundred islands having people living on them, as distinct from 'just visiting'. It has often been remarked that the main difference between the peoples of Orkney and Shetland is that the Orcadian is a farmer with a boat while the Shetlander is a fisherman with a croft. While the advent of North Sea oil has obviously brought changes to Shetland's way of life, it should not be forgotten that Shetland's centuries-old position at a cross-roads of the seas north of Britain has meant that it has always been a more cosmopolitan place than mainlanders might think.

The biggest island in Shetland is Mainland, some fifty miles long and with a coast so indented that its width varies from about 20 miles to just a few yards. On Mainland are Shetland's capital, Lerwick, and the great North Sea oil terminal of Sullom Voe. Other islands in the Shetland group are Foula in the west, Whalsay, Out Skerries and Bressay off the east coast of Mainland, and Unst, Yell and Fetlar to the north-east. High cliffs and fjords (called 'voes' here) give much of Shetland's coasts a rugged excitement, while away from the coasts much of the land is peat upland, dotted with lochs. Even this far north, in the same latitude as south Greenland, the Gulf Stream influences the climate of Shetland, making frost infrequent and letting snow lie on an average of only 15 days a winter: the snow storms of Christmas 1995 which hit Shetland with great severity may not have raised this average much, for it was 45 years since Shetland had experienced weather so severe.

The reasons for Scotland's islands falling into such a west-and-north pattern lie far back in pre-history. Some 250 million years ago, when Britain and Ireland were being formed out of the stretching and breaking apart of the huge landmass which eventually broke into North America, Greenland and Europe, the land which became Britain began to fracture along its north-western edge into what became after 200 million years or so a series of blocks of rock, some higher than others. The broken pattern of the land was then fractured still further by the actions of many volcanoes, sited in the sea near the island of Lewis and on St Kilda, Skye, Rhum, Mull and Arran; the ruined shapes of these volcanoes make up most of the landmass of the smaller islands today, while the jagged peaks of the Cuillins on Skye are reminders of volcanic action in the distant past.

While you need to have a geologist's trained eye to see signs of how Scotland's islands were formed, it is much easier to see signs of the peoples who lived here after the volcanic activity and land shifts had quietened down. (They haven't ceased: the North Atlantic is still increasing in width by a few centimetres every year.) Scattered through Scotland's islands, especially in Shetland, Orkney and the Outer Hebrides, are many remains of people from the Stone, Bronze and Iron Ages.

North Uist has, near Lochmaddy, the finest chambered cairn in the Hebrides. Called Barpa Langass, the great pile of stones was built on the side of Ben Langass by the Beaker people of the Bronze Age and included a tunnel leading into a communal burial chamber.

Lewis, also in the Outer Hebrides, has, in the impressive Standing Stones of Callanish, a monument unique in Scotland and equalled in the rest of Britain only by Stonehenge on Salisbury Plain. It was only in the middle of the 19th century that archaeologists, digging away the deep layer of peat that had built up round the stones on this ritual site, discovered just how tall they had been when they were set up in a cross pattern somewhere about 1500 BC. The tallest megalith at Callanish is more than 4.6 metres (15 feet) high. It was set up beside a cairn in the centre of a circle of thirteen stones, the circle itself being approached by an avenue of nineteen stones.

North of the Standing Stones of Callanish, south of Loch Carloway, is Dun Carloway, a well-preserved broch, or Iron Age defensive round tower. There is enough of this broch left to give a good idea of the size and style of these buildings, unique to Scotland. Archaeologists have identified the sites of about 500 brochs in Scotland, the best preserved of all of which is the one on Mousa, a small island off Shetland's Mainland. It is just a short boat trip from the pier at Leebotten, on the road to Sumburgh Head and Shetland's main airport, to Mousa, but the feeling that they have travelled far back in time is strong for many as they gaze upon the Mousa broch, standing nearly 50 feet tall on the edge of the sea. Mousa shows very well the brochs' unique double wall construction, tapering in thickness from 3.7 to 2.1 metres (12 to 7 feet). Mousa still has galleries and

stairways inside and it is possible to walk round the top, looking out to sea and across to Mainland in the same way that Picts and Norsemen did so many centuries ago.

Shetland has an even more important archaeological site at Jarlshof, just a short distance from the southern end of Sumburgh Airport's main runway. The site is, in fact, mis-named; it was Sir Walter Scott's idea, looking for something romantic to put in one of his novels, to give a Norse name to this site, even though it dates from the Bronze Age, and would seem to have been occupied by different peoples over a period of 3000 years.

Jarlshof is spread over a three-acre area of green headland, with fine views over a bay edged with a sandy beach. Archaeologists have uncovered in this relatively small area relics of the

Bronze and Iron Ages, including dwellings and even a cattle stall, of the Picts and of the Norsemen. The ovals of stone huts were preserved in the sand, as were many pieces of Neolithic pottery, stone and bone implements, bronze swords and axes. Evidence has been uncovered to suggest that the northern Picts occupied the site, while the remains of the Norse settlement which grew up here between the 9th and 14th centuries are among the most complete so far found in Britain. No wonder that archaeologists, including those working for government departments, consider Jarlshof one of Britain's most important archeological sites. one of the most important archaeological sites in Britain.

Orkney, too, has many important prehistoric remains. Indeed, you do not have to drive too far out of Stromness, once a major northern Scottish

PAGE 70
Brightly painted houses on the quayside at Tobermory, some of them dating from the 18th century, are reflected in the calm waters of the harbour. Tobermory is a fishing port and Mull's main centre.

PAGE 71
The hamlet of Brekkon, on Yell, second largest of the Shetland islands and a twenty-minute car ferry trip away from Mainland.

PAGES 72-3
Uig Sands, on the west coast of Lewis, in the Outer Hebrides. Uig, one of the four parishes into which Lewis is divided, was the scene of the discovery in 1831 of the famous 'Uig', or 'Lewis' chessmen, carved out of walrus ivory and thought to have been hidden at Uig by nuns from a Benedictine nunnery which once existed here.

ABOVE
The Standing Stones of Callanish, on Lewis, rank among the most important prehistoric sites in Scotland and date back to at least 1500 BC. In all, there are 48 stones, most of them tall and slender, set up on the moorland on the western side of Lewis. There is a central ring of stones, 37 feet in diameter, with 14 lines and one avenue of stones radiating out from the ring.

ABOVE
The Skye bridge, opened in 1995 to replace the old car ferry which for many years took motor traffic the short trip from Kyle of Lochalsh on the mainland to Kyleakin on Skye.

PAGE 78
The volcanic origins of Rhum are clearly visible in the conical shapes of its jagged peaks, seen on the horizon in this photograph, taken from the coast of Morar on the mainland. Rhum, inhabited since at least 6000 BC, lost its whole population during the Clearances and is now owned by the Nature Conservancy Council, who welcome day visitors and summer campers.

PAGE 79
Puffins in Shetland. The enormously varied bird population of Shetland, including seabirds, northern European birds and migrants, attracts visitors from all over the world. While the bird life may be observed on cliffs all over the Shetland group, there are two particularly interesting nature reserves, at Hermaness and Noss. The Hermaness National Nature Reserve on Unst is one the most important seabird sanctuaries in Britain.

port and today the ferry terminal on the west coast of Mainland, to find reminders of the presence of man from the Stone Age to the early Christian era in Britain – that is, some 4000 years of occupation – scattered over the land. The country round Loch of Stenness is particularly rich in prehistoric remains, including chambered cairns and stone circles. The great cairn of Maes Howe, generally considered to be the finest chambered tomb surviving in Europe, and thought to have been built for a line of chiefs about 1500 BC, is quite close to the main road between Kirkwall and

Stromness, and has been carefully excavated and looked after. The largest of the stone circles surviving near Maes Howe is the Ring of Brodgar, its twenty-seven remaining stones set on a bleak tongue of land separating Loch of Stenness from Loch of Harray a mile to the north of Maes Howe.

Of even greater interest, because it gives more than a hint of the way the people of these far-off times actually lived, is the remains of a whole Stone Age settlement, Skara Brae, on the Bay of Skail, about seven miles north of Stromness. Probably among the oldest

archaeological sites in Orkney, Skara Brae has been dated to 3000 BC. It is thought to have survived because over the centuries it was buried in sand. A great storm in 1850 blew away enough of the sand to reveal 'houses' linked by passages and still containing signs of their hearths, fish pools and stone beds.

At the north-western corner of Mainland, on Brough Head, is a more recent historic site, the early Christian and Norse settlement of Brough of Birsay. Here, the 20-century traveller comes face to face with the fact that until a mere five

centuries ago, Orkney and Shetland (as well as, for a time, the Hebrides and large parts of mainland Scotland and pieces of Ireland) belonged to Norway. Tired of being raided along his western coasts by Vikings based in Orkney and Shetland, Harold Haarfagr, king of Norway, took over the islands in 875. From this time until 1468, when Christian I of Norway pledged the islands as part of the dowry of his daughter, Margaret, on her marriage to James III, Orkney and Shetland were governed by Norse earls of Orkney. From about the mid-13th century, however, the earls

were all Scots, the Norse influence having been waning gradually, especially after the deaths of the two Norse earls, Magnus and Rognvald, who were canonized because of their great works as Christians.

The 11th-century Norse earl of Orkney, Thorfinn the Mighty, had his great hall at Brough of Birsay and he built a church, Christ Church, on the foundations of an earlier Celtic church nearby. The ruins of both may still be seen today, provided the tide is out and the visitor can walk across the causeway to the tidal island where Earl Thorfinn based himself. Thorfinn is known to have defeated Duncan of Scotland in battle, and he may also have sided with Macbeth after Duncan's murder.

With such a Norse heritage, it should not be surprising that a decidedly non-English and non-Scots cadence remains in the language of these islands and that a Norse influence should be apparent in place names, architecture, the law and even in local festivals. Lerwick's far-famed fire festival, Up-Helly-Aa, which takes place at the end of January every year and involves the burning of a Viking long ship, is a direct reference to Shetland's Norse heritage. Orkney's annual 'Ba' Game', 'played' round Kirkwall's Mercat Cross every New Year's Day by those

who have survived Hogmanay is certainly wild enough to have its origins in a piratical Viking and Norse past.

A different language survives in the Hebrides, too. This is Gaelic, once the main language of most of Scotland which was brought into the country by Irish settlers, but which is now confined largely to the Hebrides and remote corners of the Highlands. Even here, very few people speak only Gaelic, for English, albeit spoken with distinctive Scottish accents, is the language of the country.

While many people are attracted to Scotland's islands because of their remoteness from the tumult of modern life and for their close-knit way of life, often based on crofting — that is, the subsistence farming of agriculturally poor land combined with other forms of making an income, such as fishing, weaving, crafts and tourism — others come for the outdoor activities, whether walking, climbing in the Black Cuillins, sailing, or sea angling and loch and river fishing, and for the islands' superb natural history. The islands' very remoteness and the fact that they are cut off from the mainland has given them a rich and often unique wildlife and an interesting flora.

Birds are, of course, a main attraction, with

spectacular sites for migrating, visiting and nesting birds attracting bird watchers from all over the world, often to well-established nature reserves, such as the Balranald Nature Reserve on North Uist or to South Uist's Loch Druidibeg National Nature Reserve, which is Britain's most important breeding ground for the greylag goose.

Seals are a common sight round most islands and even otters are regular sights on many. Numerous islands, on the other hand, have species and types of animals unique to themselves. Shetland has its ponies, as does Rhum, while both Rhum and St Kilda can boast of an unique type of mouse, evolved from a mainland type long isolated from its origins. The St Kilda group has had for at least a thousand years the small, dark brown Soay sheep, a primitive breed directly descended from Neolithic root stock. North Ronaldsay, too, has a breed of short-tailed sheep which feeds largely on seaweed, so that its dark-coloured meat has a uniquely rich flavour, though this would probably not over-impress the inhabitants of Lewis, who believe that the heather cropped by their sheep gives the meat a particularly delicious flavour.

Scotland and North Sea Oil

including the great west coast yards at Ardyne Point, Hunterston, Loch Kishorn and Portavadie, other bases, at Lerwick, Wick, Peterhead, Montrose and Dundee, have all grown to continue supplying and servicing the great rigs which rise like small, brightly-lit space-age islands from the stormy water of the North Sea.

Drilling began on the first exploratory oil well the North Sea in 1964, with the first well to be drille in Scottish waters started in 1967. British Petroleum (BP) found the first big oil field, the Forties Field, 100 miles east of Aberdeen in 1970. Within two years, the North Sea was recognized as one of the world's major oil production areas and by the early 1990s some 50 oil fields and 25 gas fields were in production. The discovery in 1993 of a significant new reserve in the North Sea west of the Shetland Islands – hitherto, the main fields were in the sector east of the Shetlands – ensured that the Shetlands would retain an important role in North Sea oil production for years to come.

While few areas of Scotland's life, social, political, financial, industrial and even academic, have been quite untouched by the discovery of oil i the North Sea, its greatest outward effects have bee felt in Shetland, Orkney and along Scotland's north eastern seaboard, particularly in Aberdeen, whose Dyce airport includes the busiest heliport in the world. In Shetland, the great oil terminal at Sullom Voe – a Norse name meaning 'a place in the sun' – now takes in oil via two pipelines from North Sea fields whose names, including Magnus, Thistle, Brent, Ninian and others, have become as familiar a many place names on the mainland. Gas from these fields as well as from fields further south, east of Aberdeen, is piped to St Fergus and Cruden Bay north of Aberdeen on the mainland and on down to Mossmorran and Braefoot Bay on the Firth of Fort Orkney also has an oil pipeline terminal at Flotta, taking oil from the Piper, Tartan and Claymore field which lie in the North Sea east of the northernmost tip of the Scottish mainland.

Oil has given Scotland a technologically advanced, highly efficient industry, directly employing or underwriting the jobs of some 100,00 people. While this has not been enough to offset entirely the terrible loss of jobs in other once-vital traditional heavy industries like ship-building, engineering and steel production, it has still been a great asset to the Scottish economy. As new fields a discovered further out and deeper down in the bed the North Sea and as technology advances to cope with the new conditions, so there will be a long-continuing need for a large supply and service industry on the mainland and on many of Scotland northern islands.

North Sea oil brought many changes to Scotland. Early in its production the changes were startlingly obvious: the spindly, space-age shapes of not yet completed steel production platforms began to rise on the horizon beyond towns like Nairn and Inverness, at Nigg Bay in Cromarty and Methil in Fife; round on the west coast at Loch Kishorn and Ardyne Point in Argyll the first reinforced concrete gravity platforms were constructed; supply bases began to take shape at Dundee and Aberdeen; manufacturers in the south round Glasgow and Edinburgh stepped up production of cranes, compressors, pumps and generators; roads were upgraded and airports, especially at Aberdeen and Inverness, were extended.

While the changing nature of the industry has meant that many of the yards where the huge production platforms were built have now closed,